FLEETWOOD MAℂ

The Complete Recording Sessions
1967–1997

FLEETWOOD MAC

The Complete Recording Sessions
1967–1997

PETER LEWRY

BLANDFORD

This book is dedicated to
all the members of Fleetwood Mac
past and present

A BLANDFORD BOOK

First published in the UK 1998 by Blandford
a Cassell imprint
Cassell plc
Wellington House
125 Strand
London WC2R 0BB
www.cassell.co.uk

Distributed in the United States by Sterling Publisher Co., Inc., 387 Park Avenue South, New York, NY 10016-8810

A Cataloguing-in-Publication Data entry for this title is available from the British Library

ISBN 0-7137-2724-1

Designed by Chris Bell

Printed and bound in Great Britain by The Bath Press, Bath

title page *The most successful line-up of the band in 1975.*

previous page *Fleetwood Mac in 1979, taken from the back of the* Tusk *album.*

Contents

Foreword by Bob Brunning   7

Preface   8
     How to use the book   9

Acknowledgements   10

Introduction   12

THE BLUES YEARS 1967–1968   15

THEN PLAY ON 1969–1973   37

HEROES ARE HARD TO FIND 1974–1975   57

YESTERDAY'S GONE 1976–1980   63

NOT JUST A MIRAGE 1981–1990   75

NEVER BREAK THE CHAIN 1991–1997   89

Recording Technology   96

Recording Terminology   100

Fleetwood Mac Biographies   101

Complete Discography   107

Chart Statistics   119

Awards   121

Song Title Index   123

Foreword

IT HARDLY SEEMS POSSIBLE that it is over thirty years ago that I nervously stepped on to the stage at the Windsor Jazz & Blues Festival in August 1967 with Fleetwood Mac. There were just four of us: Peter Green, Mick Fleetwood, Jeremy Spencer and me. We were virtually bottom of the bill, but nevertheless very grateful . . . and terrified . . . to be there. None of us could have known what the future held for the Mac (well, apart from me. I knew I was a temporary member until John McVie came aboard two months later!)

The band played on, surviving some astonishing set-backs during the next three decades. Members came and went amid dramas and traumas. However, if ever the word resilient could be applied to any Mac members, then Messrs McVie and Fleetwood are the ones. They quite simply NEVER gave up! Lesser men would have quit ten times over, but their faith in Fleetwood Mac never let them down. Their gritty determination paid off when their discovery of the talented but hungry and unsuccessful L.A. musicians Stevie Nicks and Lindsey Buckingham led to the recording of one of the world's top selling albums, RUMOURS. A musical saga of the Fleetwood Mac soap opera if ever there was!

Of course, true to form, that classic line-up also tore itself apart, but not before producing some truly memorable music, including TUSK and TANGO IN THE NIGHT.

The period between 1990 and 1996 was a little less productive, but 1997 saw Lindsey and Stevie rejoin Christine, John McVie and Mick Fleetwood to recreate arguably the strongest ever Mac line-up.

But perhaps the best news, as this book goes to press, is that the talented founder of Fleetwood Mac, guitarist Peter Green, appears to be making a tremendous recovery from the illness which dogged him from the seventies to the nineties. Out on the road with his band and receiving popular acclaim, Peter is regaining his love of music. There will not be any member of the Mac, past or present, who will not celebrate this, just the latest development in the life of one of the most popular and controversial bands in the world: Fleetwood Mac.

Bob Brunning

Preface

THE MAIN PART of this book is the wealth of material recorded by Fleetwood Mac. This, I hope, will be the definitive work for those who want to know the full story of the music, as recorded by Fleetwood Mac.

I have attempted to present all the facts about what was recorded although there are many unresolved questions upon which this book cannot throw light. It is unclear how many tapes are stored at the vaults at Warner/Reprise although it is believed that there are hours of live material that was recorded during the group's 1979/80 'Tusk' tour.

I have tracked down as much information as possible on each and every recording and pieced it together, along with quotes and accompanying text, in order to present a clear and detailed analysis of the music of Fleetwood Mac.

How to use the book

The book is split into six main chapters. Each chapter will follow the group's career with biographical information, quotes and detailed session data. Each session is dealt with under the following four main headings:

1 Identification of the session
For whom the sessions were recorded
Recording date of session
Location of session, i.e. studio/venue

2 Tracks recorded
Song title (with take number where known)
Single/album where track first appeared

3 Musicians
Instrument played followed by musician

4 Studio personnel
Producer(s)
Engineer(s)
Additional information on session

Unfortunately the information on the sessions is not always complete and in these rare instances a dash (—) will be added to the blank spaces. It cannot be determined if the unissued material listed throughout the book is finished masters, out-takes, false starts or just unsuitable for release.

The book contains a complete UK/US discography of, mainly, first releases detailing singles, albums as well as selected bootlegs, videos and a list of albums released by solo members of the group. Also included is an interesting insight to the recording technology by Mike Ross-Trevor and a technical index where certain recording terms are explained.

Additional sections include individual group member biographies, chart statistics, awards and an A–Z song-title index.

Acknowledgements

THIS BOOK COULD never have been written without the help and support of many people and special thanks go to: Mike Ross; Mike Vernon; Bob Brunning; Sarah Blakely and Phil Savill at Sony Music Entertainment (UK); Richard Bowe at Sony Music Archives; Andy Linehan at the National Sound Archive; Lisa and Marty Adelson; Aine Foley; All Action Celebrity Photos; Nancy Barr-Brandon; Kaylee Coxall at the British Phonographic Institute; Bob Harvey at the Record Industry Association of America; Shivohn at Sound City Studios; Michael Bise; Carole Lewry; Peter Moody; Nigel Goodall; Rosie Anderson and my editor Stuart Booth at Cassell.

Special thanks are due to Nancy Barr-Brandon for the photographs on the following pages: 66, 68, 82, 91 (right). (Photographs available from: 506 Windermere Avenue, Interlaken, NJ 07712, USA)

References

I consulted the following books and periodicals during my research:

Brunning, Bob, *Fleetwood Mac – Behind the Masks*, New English Library, 1990

Carr, Roy, and Clarke, Steve, *Fleetwood Mac: Rumours 'n' Fax*, Harmony Books, 1978

Clemins, Martin, *Peter Green the Biography*, Castle Communications, 1995

Fleetwood, Mick, *Fleetwood: My Life and Adventures with Fleetwood Mac*, Sidgwick & Jackson, 1990

— *My Twenty-Five Years in Fleetwood Mac*, Weidenfeld & Nicholson, 1992

Frame, Pete, *The Complete Rock Family Trees*, Omnibus, 1993

Gambaccini, Paul; Rice, Tim, and Rice, Jonathan, *The Guinness Book of Hit Singles*, Guinness Publications, 1997

— *The Guinness Book of Hit Albums*, Guinness Publications, 1997

Garner, Ken, *In Session,Tonight*, BBC Books, 1993

Graham, Samuel, *The Authorized History of Fleetwood Mac*, Warner Bros Publications Ltd, 1978

Newman, Richard, *John Mayall Bluesbreaker*, Castle Communications, 1995

Rees, Dafydd, and Crampton, Luke, *The Guinness Book of Rock Stars*, Guinness Publications, 1994

Whitburn, Joel, *The Billboard Book of Top Forty Albums*, Billboard Books, 1995

— *The Billboard Book of Top Forty Singles*, Billboard Books, 1995

Magazines/periodicals:
Record Collector
MOJO
New Musical Express
Melody Maker
Billboard
Rolling Stone
Q

I would also like to make mention of the following fan clubs and Internet pages that provided me with valuable information:

'**Crystal**': Aine Foley, 46 St John's Avenue, Clondalkin, Dublin 22, Ireland
Penguin: http://www.cyberpenguin.net/penguin/
Fleetwood Mac Legacy: http://vrienden.pandora.be/dirk.faes/

Introduction

FLEETWOOD MAC – the name has always stood for high quality rock and roll. Their mix of black American roots and English restlessness evolved into a blues movement the impact of which would be felt all over the world. They were at the forefront of the British blues movement of the late sixties.

Founded by drummer Mick Fleetwood, bassist John McVie, and talented guitarist Peter Green, they were later joined by fellow guitarists Jeremy Spencer and Danny Kirwan. Established in Britain with a string of ground-breaking hits like 'Need Your Love So Bad', 'Albatross', 'Black Magic Woman' and 'Oh Well' the three singer-instrumentalist frontline soon gained a reputation for constant growth and change.

Over the years Green, Spencer and Kirwan would all leave the group to be replaced by new members Christine McVie, Bob Welch, Bob Weston and Dave Walker with each new person playing an important role in the musical direction of the group. Leaving the pure blues behind them they recorded in various styles – jazz, country, rock 'n' roll and rhythm and blues. Despite these changes the band survived and prospered. They released THEN PLAY ON, KILN HOUSE, BARE TREES, FUTURE GAMES and PENGUIN as well as undertaking a never-ending round of live performances in their home country as well as America, Europe and Scandinavia. Bob Welch's decision to leave the band in 1974 and the discovery of Stevie Nicks and Lindsey Buckingham would launch an era in the group's history that would last for over a decade and bring unprecedented success.

With Buckingham and Nicks the group returned to the three front-person line-up that had brought them success in the past. It was the release of RUMOURS in 1977 that gave Fleetwood Mac the level of success that earned them their superstar tag. With record sales in excess of 35 million worldwide and with over 31 weeks at number one it produced four top ten hits and a Grammy Award. TUSK, FLEETWOOD MAC LIVE and MIRAGE were all further confirmation of their position as one of the most creative bands in rock 'n' roll.

The 1987 release TANGO IN THE NIGHT saw a band with years of experience, both alone and together, produce an album with emotion, technological brilliance and polish. A top-ten hit in ten countries, the

Recent photo of Fleetwood Mac's founder – Peter Green.

multi-platinum album produced six hit singles. Lindsey Buckingham's decision to quit the band followed the release of TANGO IN THE NIGHT and two new members, Rick Vito and Billy Burnette, were brought in to replace him. Their first album together was the 1990 release BEHIND THE MASK. The 1995 album TIME saw another line-up for the group. Ex-Traffic guitarist Dave Mason and Bekka Bramlett, daughter of Delaney & Bonnie, replaced Stevie Nicks and Rick Vito on their departure.

In 1997 the RUMOURS line-up re-formed for an MTV special, released on CD and video as THE DANCE, and undertook a forty-date tour of the US.

They have earned respect worldwide for their hard work and *'do what feels right, but do it well'* approach to music, an attitude that has kept them evolving for over thirty years. The story isn't over yet, it continues to be written. Fleetwood Mac are a special band – and this is their musical history.

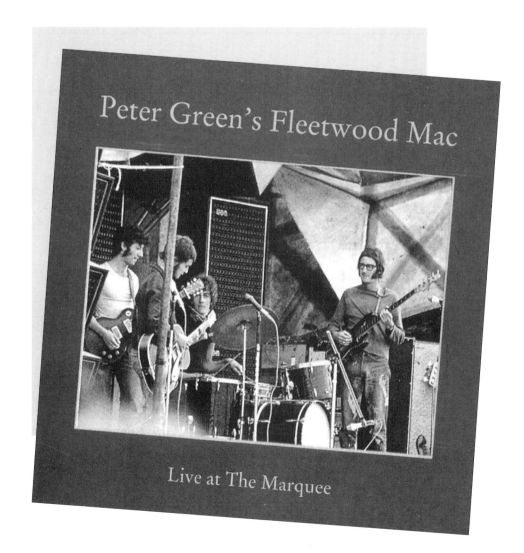

CD cover for LIVE AT THE MARQUEE *album.*

THE BLUES YEARS
1967–1968

THE BRITISH BLUES boom of the mid-sixties, helped along by appearances of American blues legends like Muddy Waters, saw the formation of many bands who were bringing the music of the American South to a much wider audience. Of the many groups to emerge during this time two stand out and will be written into the annals of popular music – John Mayall's Bluesbreakers and Peter Green's Fleetwood Mac. John Mayall had previously been in the Manchester-based group Blues Syndicate, and in 1966 formed the Bluesbreakers, whose early line-up included Jack Bruce and Eric Clapton. Mayall's BLUESBREAKERS album was the first British blues album to achieve any sort of commercial success. When Eric Clapton and Jack Bruce left to form Cream, John Mayall turned to Peter Green as a replacement. During his time with Mayall he appeared on just the one album, A HARD ROAD and a handful of singles. When Green joined the Bluesbreakers, John McVie had already been in the band for nearly three years and, after the departure of drummer Aynsley Dunbar in April 1967, the roots of a new group were formed with the induction of Mick Fleetwood. Legend has it that as a present for Green, who was celebrating his birthday, Mayall paid for some studio time and this line-up recorded two singles and an instrumental, which would remain unissued for four years. This was 'Fleetwood Mac', the name derived from Peter Green's favourite rhythm section.

STUDIO SESSION FOR DECCA
19 April 1967
Decca Studios, West Hampstead

Double Trouble	A-side
It Hurts Me Too	B-side
Fleetwood Mac	THE ORIGINAL FLEETWOOD MAC
First Train Home	THE ORIGINAL FLEETWOOD MAC

Guitar: Peter Green
Vocal/Piano/Guitar: John Mayall
Bass: John McVie
Drums: Mick Fleetwood

Producer: Mike Vernon
Engineer: Gus Dudgeon

JOHN MCVIE: *I had been playing in a Shadows-style group and I knew nothing at all about blues music. Mayall just gave me a stack of records and asked me to listen to them to see if I could grasp the style and feeling. The first gig I did with him was at the White Hart, Acton… he said 'OK let's try a 12 bar in C' and I had to ask him what he meant. He just told me to follow his chords, and over the months I began to learn what the blues was about.* (The Complete Rock Family Trees)

MICK FLEETWOOD: *The only time I ever stopped drumming was after I left the Shotgun Express: I did a bit of interior decorating with a friend.* (The Complete Rock Family Trees)

JOHN MCVIE: *I've only ever played in two groups in my life: John Mayall's Bluesbreakers and Fleetwood Mac. I joined Mayall in January 1963 when he moved down to London from Manchester where he'd been flogging around for years – always playing the same kind of blues rooted music.*
(The Complete Rock Family Trees)

The Green, McVie and Fleetwood line-up only lasted a few weeks. Mick Fleetwood was fired for excessive drinking and Green left after a disagreement with Mayall. John McVie would stay with the group for several more months. In July 1967 Fleetwood Mac were formed. At this stage John McVie was yet to leave the security of the Bluesbreakers and the line-up consisted of Peter Green on vocals/guitar, Mick Fleetwood on drums, Bob Brunning on bass and Jeremy Spencer, who had been recommended to Green by Mike Vernon, on vocals and guitar.

MIKE VERNON: *You know how sometimes you can tell when the writing's on the wall? Well, it was a bit like that with the relationship between Mayall and Green. John really rated Peter's playing as well as his vocal prowess. I don't know if he was aware of his talents as a harp player too but possibly not. Peter kept telling me he was fed-up with the Bluesbreakers set-up and really wanted to put his own unit together. When he recorded that instrumental on the same day as two other titles with Mayall and told me to put 'Fleetwood Mac' on the box label I knew something was afoot. During the following weeks and months he kept dropping hints with regard to my fanzine label Blue Horizon. Need I say more?*

Mike Vernon was the house producer for Decca who worked on many of John Mayall's recordings. He was also running a small independent blues label, Purdah. Along with his brother Richard he started Blue Horizon records in 1967, and, impressed with his label, Green formed Fleetwood Mac and signed to Blue Horizon. Vernon also auditioned the Birmingham-based blues outfit The Levi-Set and, although he did not sign them up, was impressed with the playing of their guitarist

Jeremy Spencer, an Elmore James fanatic and sound-alike, and recommended him to Green who had found the last piece of his musical jigsaw.

BOB BRUNNING: *I joined Fleetwood Mac by accident. The ad in Melody Maker just said 'bass player wanted for Chicago type blues band', so along I went and told Peter Green that he had the 'right name for a guitar player' considering how good his namesake was in John Mayall's Bluesbreakers. He soon put me right, I felt a complete idiot, but still got the job!. . . Of course, it was a great thrill for me to be in the studio with such a wonderful band. I'd recorded before: my college band Five's Company had produced three singles for Pye Records, but Fleetwood Mac were something else! Peter Green was very helpful to me. He was an accomplished bass player himself and gave me plenty of good advice and free tuition.*

MICK FLEETWOOD: *A few weeks after I'd been ejected from the Bluesbreakers, Peter Green gave in his notice. . . he'd had enough. His initial plans didn't involve forming a new band, but his agency persuaded him, and he came round to see me. . . and between us, we got Fleetwood Mac together. At the time we had no manager, so we did everything ourselves – got the van and the equipment sorted out – and Peter did all the negotiation with Blue Horizon Records. In fact it was Mike Vernon of Blue Horizon who suggested Jeremy Spencer: he was playing in a blues band called The Levi Set – so Peter went up to Birmingham, saw him in action, and asked him to join us. . . whereupon we started rehearsing to prepare for our debut at Windsor.*
(The Complete Rock Family Trees)

And what a debut. . . !

The Windsor Jazz & Blues Festival was held over three days in August at the Windsor Racecourse and Fleetwood Mac appeared on the Sunday night finale. Headlined by Cream, the Jeff Beck Group and John Mayall's Bluesbreakers a very nervous Fleetwood Mac played a 20-minute set before a crowd of 30,000 people. They also played a set at a 'fringe' festival later in the evening.

In September they made their first recordings at the Decca Studios in West Hampstead. With Mike Vernon producing, they recorded two tracks both destined to become the B-sides of their debut singles in both the UK and US. Jeremy Spencer did not play on this session.

right Music press advertisement for the Windsor Jazz & Blues Festival.

below The original Fleetwood Mac line-up at their debut performance at the Windsor Jazz & Blues Festival, 13 August 1967.

STUDIO SESSION FOR BLUE HORIZON
September 1967
Decca Studios, West Hampstead

Rambling Pony	B-side
Long Grey Mare	B-side (US)/PETER GREEN'S FLEETWOOD MAC

Vocal/Guitar/Harmonica: Peter Green
Bass: Bob Brunning
Drums: Mick Fleetwood

Producer: Mike Vernon
Engineer: Gus Dudgeon or Roy Thomas-Baker

Early studio shot featuring Jeremy Spencer,
Mick Fleetwood, Bob Brunning and Peter Green.

STUDIO SESSION FOR BLUE HORIZON
9 September 1967
CBS Studios, New Bond Street, London

I Believe My Time Ain't Long (Take 1)	A-side
Rambling Pony # 2 (Take 1)	THE ORIGINAL FLEETWOOD MAC

Vocal/Guitar/Harmonica: Peter Green
Guitar: Jeremy Spencer
Bass: Bob Brunning
Drums: Mick Fleetwood

Producer: Mike Vernon
Engineer: Mike Ross

Session note: Overdubs were carried out on these two tracks.

Paperwork from the September 1967 sessions. This tape was later used for the recording of 'Need Your Love So Bad.'

These two sessions were the only appearance, on an official release of the original line-up of the group with Bob Brunning on bass. At the end of September John McVie would finally quit the Bluesbreakers and replace Bob in Fleetwood Mac.

Regular appearances at the famed Marquee Club in London's Wardour Street followed and a recording of the original line-up of the group has made an appearance on an unofficial CD. Their set included a number of covers of blues standards including Elmore James' 'I Held My Baby Last Night', 'Got To Move' and 'Dust My Blues', a reworking of 'Dust My Broom', along with some of their own compositions including Green's 'Watch Out' and 'Looking For Somebody'.

BOB BRUNNING: *I was very pleased to receive in 1986 from a German collector a live tape of the complete performance of Fleetwood Mac at the Marquee on September 15, 1967, the band's second gig. Remember, these were pre-Sony Walkman days, and the enthusiastic but anonymous fan must have been lumbered with a cumbersome battery operated reel-to-reel tape recorder! The quality is not exactly digital, but the tape does provide a fascinating record of the very first Fleetwood Mac line-up.*

Discernible through the lo-fi fog is Peter Green's stunning playing, clearly illustrating his burgeoning talent.

LIVE RECORDING
15 September 1967
Marquee Club, Wardour Street, London

Talk To Me Baby	LIVE AT THE MARQUEE
I Held My Baby Last Night	LIVE AT THE MARQUEE
My Baby's Sweet	LIVE AT THE MARQUEE
Looking For Somebody	LIVE AT THE MARQUEE
Evil Woman Blues	LIVE AT THE MARQUEE
Got To Move	LIVE AT THE MARQUEE
No Place To Go	LIVE AT THE MARQUEE
Watch Out	LIVE AT THE MARQUEE
Mighty Long Time	LIVE AT THE MARQUEE
Dust My Blues	LIVE AT THE MARQUEE
I Need You, Come On Home	LIVE AT THE MARQUEE
Shake Your Moneymaker	LIVE AT THE MARQUEE

Vocal/Guitar/Harmonica: Peter Green
Guitar: Jeremy Spencer
Bass: Bob Brunning
Drums: Mick Fleetwood

Producer: —
Engineer: —

Session note: There is some doubt as to the correct location and date of this recording. Although the title suggests the Marquee it is possible that the tapes originate from a club date, probably in London and from later in the year.

MICK FLEETWOOD: *We made quite an auspicious debut at the Annual Windsor Jazz & Blues Festival at Windsor in August – but Bob Brunning knew he was only in the group until John McVie made his mind up. Bob didn't mind leaving – he'd earned some prestige from Fleetwood Mac, and he went off and formed his own band, which did quite well.* (The Complete Rock Family Trees)

BOB BRUNNING: *I thoroughly enjoyed my brief stint with Fleetwood Mac and remained friendly with them all. People often ask me how I feel about it. I actually got 'promotion' at the time. I joined Savoy Brown who were working three times as hard and made a lot more money. After leaving them I then formed the Brunning Sunflower Blues Band with Savoy Brown colleague Bob Hall.*

Following a string of gigs at regular blues haunts such as Cook's Ferry Inn, The 100 Club in Oxford Street and the White Hart in Acton, Fleetwood Mac finally went into the studios of CBS in New Bond Street, London to begin work on their first album. The resulting LP PETER GREEN'S FLEETWOOD MAC is regarded as one of the classic British blues albums and reached number four, spending 37 weeks in the album chart. Several tracks were held over until 1971 and released on the compilation album THE ORIGINAL FLEETWOOD MAC.

MIKE VERNON: *There was an air of excitement and expectancy and thankfully never one of feeling under any pressure. Everyone did what they felt as and when they felt it. We knew we needed to make an album that would represent the band 'Live' and we felt at that time we achieved just that. We added a couple of solo acoustic numbers for variety and also made use of one of the original demo tracks. Peter's very fine Howlin' Wolf inspired harmonica work was also featured. All in all it was an album to be proud of.*

In the late sixties there was a wide audience clamouring for pop music over the airwaves, and although their appetite had been sustained by the pirate stations like Radio Caroline and Radio London it was not until late 1967 that a BBC station devoted air-time specifically to pop music. Radio 1 was not the only BBC station to be broadcasting popular music though. Radio 2, the Light Programme, the World Service and even Radio 3 all broadcast specially recorded sessions by the popular groups of the day. Most of these sessions were held at the BBC's studios in Maida Vale, London, and it was here on 7 November 1967 that Fleetwood Mac recorded their first radio session for 'Top Gear'.

SESSION FOR RADIO 1 'TOP GEAR'
7 November 1967
Maida Vale 4, London

Long Grey Mare	Radio Broadcast/ LIVE AT THE BBC
Baby Please Set A Date	Radio Broadcast/ LIVE AT THE BBC
Looking For Somebody	Radio Broadcast/ LIVE AT THE BBC
Got To Move	Radio Broadcast/ LIVE AT THE BBC
Believe My Time Ain't Long	Radio Broadcast/ LIVE AT THE BBC
A Fool No More	Radio Broadcast/ LIVE AT THE BBC

Vocal/Guitar/Harmonica: Peter Green
Guitar: Jeremy Spencer
Bass: John McVie
Drums: Mick Fleetwood

Producer: Bev Phillips
Engineer: Pete Ritzema

Broadcast on 12 November 1967

One half of a great rhythm section – Mick Fleetwood . . .

. . . and the other half – John McVie.

STUDIO SESSION FOR BLUE HORIZON
22 November 1967
CBS Studios, New Bond Street, London

I Loved Another Woman (Take 5)	PETER GREEN'S FLEETWOOD MAC
Merry Go Round (Take 2)	PETER GREEN'S FLEETWOOD MAC
Watch Out	THE ORIGINAL FLEETWOOD MAC
Cold Black Night (Take 6)	PETER GREEN'S FLEETWOOD MAC
The World Keep On Turning (Take 3)	PETER GREEN'S FLEETWOOD MAC
Mean Old Fireman (Take 2)	THE ORIGINAL FLEETWOOD MAC
Hellhound On My Trail (Take 2)	PETER GREEN'S FLEETWOOD MAC
A Fool No More (Take 8)	THE ORIGINAL FLEETWOOD MAC

Vocal/Guitar/Harmonica: Peter Green
Guitar/Vocal/Piano: Jeremy Spencer
Bass: John McVie
Drums: Mick Fleetwood

Producer: Mike Vernon
Engineer: Mike Ross

Session note: Several alternates exist from these sessions.

STUDIO SESSION FOR BLUE HORIZON
November–December 1967
CBS Studios, New Bond Street, London

My Heart Beat Like A Hammer	PETER GREEN'S FLEETWOOD MAC
Looking For Somebody	PETER GREEN'S FLEETWOOD MAC
No Place To Go	PETER GREEN'S FLEETWOOD MAC
My Baby's Good To Me	PETER GREEN'S FLEETWOOD MAC
Got To Move	PETER GREEN'S FLEETWOOD MAC
Can't Afford To Do It	THE ORIGINAL FLEETWOOD MAC
Allow Me One More Show	THE ORIGINAL FLEETWOOD MAC

Vocal/Guitar/Harmonica: Peter Green
Guitar/Vocal/Piano: Jeremy Spencer

Typical CBS tape boxes detailing tracks recorded on 22 November 1967.

Bass: John McVie
Drums: Mick Fleetwood

Producer: Mike Vernon
Engineer: Mike Ross

STUDIO SESSION FOR BLUE HORIZON
11 December 1967
CBS Studios, New Bond Street, London

Leaving Town Blues (Take 5)   THE ORIGINAL
                              FLEETWOOD MAC

Don't Dog Me Woman   *Unissued*
Shake Your Moneymaker   PETER GREEN'S
   (Take 1)   FLEETWOOD MAC

Vocal/Guitar/Harmonica: Peter Green
Guitar/Vocal/Piano: Jeremy Spencer
Bass: John McVie
Drums: Mick Fleetwood

Producer: Mike Vernon
Engineer: Mike Ross

MIKE ROSS: PETER GREEN'S FLEETWOOD
MAC, *the first album for Blue
Horizon, was recorded onto a four-
track machine, the complete live
performance including live vocals
with no overdubbing.*

During this period, Fleetwood Mac had
become the resident house band for Blue
Horizon, who, having signed a deal with CBS
that allowed them to release records on their
own Blue Horizon label, were signing many of
the little known blues artists. Over the coming months they would provide backing on
albums by Duster Bennet, Eddie Boyd and
Otis Spann, amongst others.

It was at their next 'Top Gear' session, in
January, that Jeremy Spencer's other musical
love was aired for the first time. It was well
known that he could recreate Elmore James
slide guitar style but what was less well docu-
mented was his love for fifties rock 'n' roll and
in particular the music of Elvis Presley and
Buddy Holly. Both 'Don't Be Cruel' and the

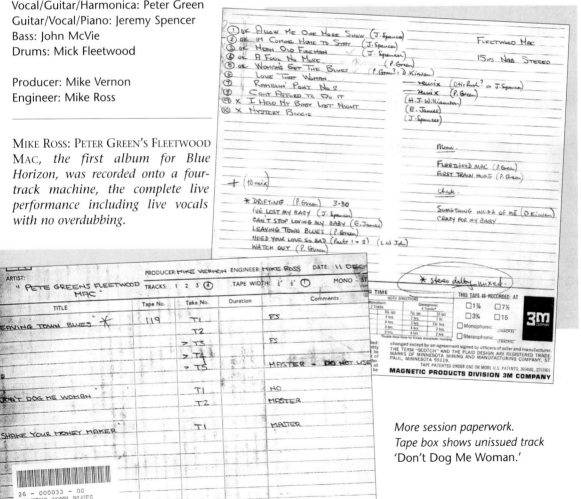

More session paperwork.
Tape box shows unissued track
'Don't Dog Me Woman.'

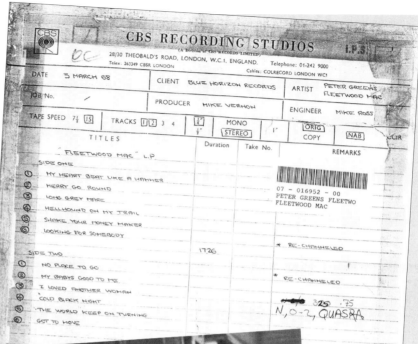

right *Master reel showing the running order for the band's first album.*

below *Classic cover of Fleetwood Mac's first album.*

amazingly titled 'Bee-I-Bicky-Bop-Blue-Jean-Honey-Babe-Meets-High-School-Hound-Dog-Hot-Rod-Man' show what an influence this music had on him – and it would not be the last time that it would be committed to tape.

SESSION FOR RADIO 1 'TOP GEAR'
16 January 1968
Aeolian Hall, Studio 2

I Can't Hold On	Radio Broadcast/
	LIVE AT THE BBC
Blue Coat Man	Radio Broadcast
Sweet Little Angel	Radio Broadcast
The Stroller	Radio Broadcast

Bee-I-Bicky-Bop-Blue-Jean-
    Honey-Babe-Meets-
    High-School-Hound-
    Dog-Hot-Rod-Man
	Radio Broadcast

Where You Belong *	Radio Broadcast
Don't Be Cruel *	Radio Broadcast
The Sun Is Shining *	Radio Broadcast
World Keeps Turning *	Radio Broadcast/
	LIVE AT THE BBC

Vocal/Guitar/Harmonica: Peter Green
Guitar: Jeremy Spencer
Bass: John McVie
Drums: Mick Fleetwood
Piano/Vocal: Eddie Boyd

Producer: Bernie Andrews
Engineer: Dave Tate

Broadcast on 21 January 1968 (except * broadcast 24 March 1968)

right Jeremy Spencer at the CBS Studios, London *during the recording of their first album.*

below Mick Fleetwood and Peter Green during a *break in recording.*

The recording of 7936 SOUTH RHODES, an album by American blues pianist Eddie Boyd that Mike Vernon was recording for release on Blue Horizon, found Fleetwood, Green and McVie, minus Spencer, working as the house band for the first time.

STUDIO SESSION FOR BLUE HORIZON
25 January 1968
CBS Studios, New Bond Street, London

You Got To Reap	7936 SOUTH RHODES
Just The Blues	7936 SOUTH RHODES
She's Real	7936 SOUTH RHODES
Back Slack	7936 SOUTH RHODES
Be Careful	7936 SOUTH RHODES
Ten To One	7936 SOUTH RHODES
The Blues Is Here To Stay	7936 SOUTH RHODES
You Are My Love	7936 SOUTH RHODES
Third Degree	7936 SOUTH RHODES
Thank You Baby	7936 SOUTH RHODES
She's Gone	7936 SOUTH RHODES
(I Can't Stop) Loving You	7936 SOUTH RHODES
The Big Boat	A-side/7936 SOUTH RHODES

Sent For You Yesterday, And Here You Come Today	B-side/7936 SOUTH RHODES

Guitar: Peter Green
Vocal/Piano: Eddie Boyd
Bass: John McVie
Drums: Mick Fleetwood

Producer: Mike Vernon
Engineer: Mike Ross

STUDIO SESSION FOR BLUE HORIZON
14 February 1968
CBS Studios, New Bond Street, London

Black Magic Woman (Take 7)	A-side
Black Magic Woman (different mix)	THE BLUE HORIZON STORY 1965-1970 VOL. 1

Vocal/Guitar/Harmonica: Peter Green
Guitar: Jeremy Spencer
Bass: John McVie
Drums: Mick Fleetwood

Producer: Mike Vernon
Engineer: Mike Ross

Tape box showing 2nd stage master production of 'Black Magic Woman'. Note that material by other artists was also worked on during the same day.

Destined to become the group's second single, 'Black Magic Woman' demonstrated Green's developing talent as a songwriter. With its sinister guitar playing and confident vocal it should have been a much bigger hit deserving better than its high of number 37 in the charts.

SESSION FOR RADIO 3 'BLUES IN BRITAIN'
26 February 1968
Maida Vale 5, London

Where You Belong	Radio Broadcast
World Keeps Turning	*Not Broadcast*

Vocal/Guitar/Harmonica: Peter Green
Guitar: Jeremy Spencer
Bass: John McVie
Drums: Mick Fleetwood

Producer: Jeff Griffin
Engineer: —

LIVE RECORDING
April 1968
London

Got To Move	LONDON LIVE '68
I Held My Baby Last Night	LONDON LIVE '68
My Baby's Sweet	LONDON LIVE '68
My Baby's A Good 'Un	LONDON LIVE '68
Don't Know Which Way To Go	LONDON LIVE '68
Buzz Me	LONDON LIVE '68
The Dream	LONDON LIVE '68
The World Keep On Turning	LONDON LIVE '68
How Blue Can You Get	LONDON LIVE '68
Bleeding Heart	LONDON LIVE '68

Vocal/Guitar/Harmonica: Peter Green
Guitar: Jeremy Spencer
Bass: John McVie
Drums: Mick Fleetwood

Producer: —
Engineer: —

This unofficial release was a good representation of the group's current stage act and featured a high percentage of otherwise unavailable material including BB King's 'Buzz Me' and 'How Blue Can I Get'.

SESSION FOR RADIO 1 'SATURDAY CLUB'
9 April 1968
Playhouse Theatre, London

Worried Dream	Radio Broadcast
Please Find My Baby	Radio Broadcast
Black Magic Woman	Radio Broadcast
Peggy Sue Got Married	Radio Broadcast

Vocal/Guitar/Harmonica: Peter Green
Guitar: Jeremy Spencer
Bass: John McVie
Drums: Mick Fleetwood

Producer: Bill Bebb
Engineer: —

Broadcast on 13 April 1968

STUDIO SESSION FOR BLUE HORIZON
11 April 1968
CBS Studios, New Bond Street, London

(When) The Sun Is Shining	B-side (UK)
Worried Dream (Take 2)	THE ORIGINAL FLEETWOOD MAC
Need Your Love So Bad	*Unissued*
Love That Woman	THE ORIGINAL FLEETWOOD MAC
Drifting	THE ORIGINAL FLEETWOOD MAC

Vocal/Guitar/Harmonica: Peter Green
Guitar: Jeremy Spencer
Bass: John McVie
Drums: Mick Fleetwood

Producer: Mike Vernon
Engineer: Mike Ross

Tape box showing the master of 'Worried Dream' and early takes of 'Need Your Love So Bad'.

The material recorded during this session, with the exception of '(When) The Sun Is Shining', the B-side of 'Black Magic Woman', and an early attempt at 'Need Your Love So Bad', would remain in the can until 1971.

SESSION FOR RADIO 1 'NIGHTRIDE'
16 April 1968
Aeolian Hall, Studio 2, London

How Blue Can You Get	Radio Broadcast
My Baby Is Sweet	Radio Broadcast
Long Grey Mare	Radio Broadcast
Buzz Me	Radio Broadcast
I'm So Lonesome And Blue	Radio Broadcast

Vocal/Guitar/Harmonica: Peter Green
Guitar: Jeremy Spencer
Bass: John McVie
Drums: Mick Fleetwood

Producer: Denis O'Keefe
Engineer: —

Broadcast on 17 April 1968

Following an extensive touring schedule that took in the Scandinavian countries as well as the UK, Fleetwood Mac turned their attentions to the important task of recording their second album. The band were keen to recreate a club sound on the album and the unenviable task was handed over to producer Mike Vernon and engineer Mike Ross.

MIKE ROSS: *The band wanted to create a club sound on these tracks so we set up some speakers in the studio, placed microphones directly in front of the speakers and recorded the tracks.*

MIKE VERNON: *They must have been some of the strangest, weirdest recording sessions of the 1960s. To get an authentic feel of Chess Studios in the 1940s, Mike Ross, the engineer and I spent a lot of time manoeuvring amplifiers and speakers around the studio to get a muddy murky sound.* (Behind The Masks)

STUDIO SESSIONS FOR BLUE HORIZON
April 1968
CBS Studios, New Bond Street, London

Coming Home	MR WONDERFUL
Rollin' Man	MR WONDERFUL
Dust My Broom	MR WONDERFUL
Love That Burns	MR WONDERFUL
Doctor Brown	MR WONDERFUL
Need Your Love Tonight	MR WONDERFUL
If You Be My Baby	MR WONDERFUL

Evenin' Boogie   MR WONDERFUL
Lazy Poker Blues   MR WONDERFUL
I've Lost My Baby   MR WONDERFUL
Trying So Hard To Forget   MR WONDERFUL

Vocal/Guitar/Harmonica: Peter Green
Guitar: Jeremy Spencer
Bass: John McVie
Drums: Mick Fleetwood
Piano: Christine Perfect
Alto Saxophone: Steve Gregory
Alto Saxophone: Dave Howard
Tenor Saxophone: Johnny Almond
Tenor Saxophone: Roland Vaughan
Harmonica (on 'Trying So Hard To Forget'):
   Duster Bennett

Producer: Mike Vernon
Engineer: Mike Ross

The recording sessions for MR WONDERFUL featured a guest artiste, the future Mrs McVie, Christine Perfect. A talented piano player and successful artist in her own right with Blue Horizon stablemates Chicken Shack she was invited to record with the band. The basic Mac line-up was also expanded with a four piece saxophone section.

STUDIO SESSION FOR BLUE HORIZON
28 April 1968
CBS Studios, New Bond Street, London

Stop Messin' Around (Take 4)   MR WONDERFUL
Stop Messin' Around (Take 5)   B-side
Need Your Love So Bad   *See session dated*
  (Re-make)   *15 May 1968*

Vocal/Guitar/Harmonica: Peter Green
Guitar: Jeremy Spencer
Bass: John McVie
Drums: Mick Fleetwood
Piano: Christine McVie
Alto Saxophone: Steve Gregory
Alto Saxophone: Dave Howard
Tenor Saxophone: Johnny Almond
Tenor Saxophone: Roland Vaughan

Producer: Mike Vernon
Engineer: Mike Ross

The two released versions of 'Stop Messin' Round' are detailed on this tape box from the 28 April 1968 session.

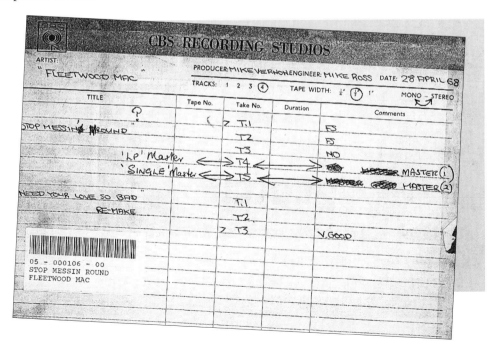

MIKE ROSS: *We recorded two versions of* 'Need Your Love So Bad'. *The first with brass and later we recorded a version with strings and brass.*

MR WONDERFUL was released in September and while it reached the top ten it did not achieve the success of the first album. The band wanted to title the album 'A Good Length' and use a different cover photo, one of the infamous 'udder' shots, but CBS gave this idea the thumbs down! Mind you the eventual cover also caused some controversy, demonstrating the groups outrageous streak, as a semi-nude Mick Fleetwood, covered strategically by some leaves, was used.

BOB BRUNNING: *I suggested the title to Peter Green during a lengthy and enjoyable meal in a Turkish restaurant in Fulham. We were fooling around after a glass or two of wine and started giggling about chat show hosts' tendency to eulogize their guests: 'the truly wonderful Mr Troy Spandex etc. etc.' I suggested to Peter that he call the album* MR WONDERFUL *and then promptly forgot all about it! But Peter didn't.*

STUDIO SESSION FOR BLUE HORIZON
15 May 1968
CBS Studios, New Bond Street, London

Need Your Love So Bad (Take 4)	A-side
Hard To Resist	*Unissued*

Vocal/Guitar/Harmonica: Peter Green
Guitar: Jeremy Spencer
Bass: John McVie
Drums: Mick Fleetwood
Piano: Christine Perfect
Alto Saxophone: Steve Gregory
Alto Saxophone: Dave Howard
Tenor Saxophone: Johnny Almond
Tenor Saxophone: Roland Vaughan

Producer: Mike Vernon
Engineer: Mike Ross

Session note: 'Need Your Love So Bad' is marked as 2nd Stage Master on the tape box. This session was probably held to overdub strings and brass onto the track.

Peter Green had heard Little Willy John's song 'Need Your Love So Bad' during his days with John Mayall. He had played BB King's version to Green and when it came time to record the track Green employed the services of Mickey

Gate-fold sleeve for MR WONDERFUL *(CD issue).*

ARTIST: "FLEETWOOD MAC" "DUSTER BENNETT"	PRODUCER: MIKE VERNON ENGINEER: MIKE ROSS DATE: 28 APRIL 15 MAY TRACKS: 1 2 3 ④ TAPE WIDTH: ¼" ½" 1" MONO – ST				
TITLE	Tape No.	Take No.	Duration		Comments
"NEED YOUR LOVE SO BAD"		T4			MASTER 2ⁿᵈ STAGE FINAL
"HARD TO RESIST" RE-MAKE		T.1			NG
		T2			NG
		T3 -			NG
		T4			NO *
	EDIT -	T5			ES
		T6			NO
		T7 -			NO
		T8			NO
		T9			√ GOOD * MASTER

'Need Your Love So Bad' *paperwork and original Blue Horizon single release.*

Baker, of Mickey & Sylvia's 'Love Is Strange' fame, to orchestrate the strings.

Their first US tour followed during which the band took time out to visit some of the Chicago blues clubs to catch some of their idols.

PETER GREEN: *I really enjoyed seeing Howlin' Wolf, Buddy Guy, Freddie King and white bluesman John Hammond.*

At the end of their US tour Fleetwood Mac returned to the UK and recorded another BBC session for broadcast on Radio 1's 'Top Gear' programme. It was at this session that they recorded their send-up of the current psychedelic sound, 'Intergalactic Musicians Walking On Velvet.'

SESSION FOR RADIO 1 'TOP GEAR'
27 May 1968
201 Piccadilly, Studio 1

That Ain't It	Radio Broadcast
Mean Mistreatin' Mama	Radio Broadcast/
	LIVE AT THE BBC
Intergalactic Musicians	
Walking On Velvet	Radio Broadcast
Dead Shrimp Blues	Radio Broadcast
Sheila *	Radio Broadcast

Vocal/Guitar/Harmonica: Peter Green
Guitar: Jeremy Spencer
Bass: John McVie
Drums: Mick Fleetwood

Producer: Bernie Andrews
Engineer: —

Broadcast on 2 June 1968 (except * broadcast 7 July 1968)

SESSION FOR RADIO 1 'TOP GEAR'
26 August 1968
201 Piccadilly, Studio 1

A Mind Of My Own	Radio Broadcast
I Have To Laugh	Radio Broadcast

Preachin' Blues	Radio Broadcast/
	LIVE AT THE BBC
You Need Love *	Radio Broadcast
A Talk With You *	Radio Broadcast
You're The One	Radio Broadcast
Bo Diddley	Radio Broadcast
Wine, Whiskey, Women *	Radio Broadcast
Crutch And Cane **	Radio Broadcast
If You Be My Baby **	Radio Broadcast
Crazy For My Baby **	Radio Broadcast
Need Your Love So Bad	Radio Broadcast

Vocal/Guitar/Harmonica: Peter Green
Guitar: Jeremy Spencer
Guitar: Danny Kirwan
Bass: John McVie
Keyboards: Christine McVie
Drums: Mick Fleetwood

Producer: Bernie Andrews
Engineer: Allen Harris

Broadcast on 1 September 1968 (except * broadcast 13 October 1968 and ** broadcast 24 November 1968)

'Shake Your Moneymaker', 'Stop Messin' Round' and 'Hawaiian Boogie' may also be from this session.

STUDIO SESSION FOR BLUE HORIZON
October 1968
CBS Studios, New Bond Street, London

Albatross	A-side
Jigsaw Puzzle Blues	B-side

Vocal/Guitar/Harmonica: Peter Green
Guitar: Danny Kirwan
Bass: John McVie
Drums: Mick Fleetwood

Producer: Mike Vernon
Engineer: Mike Ross

Session note: The tape box from this session shows 'Albatross' written as 'The Albatross' by engineer Mike Ross.

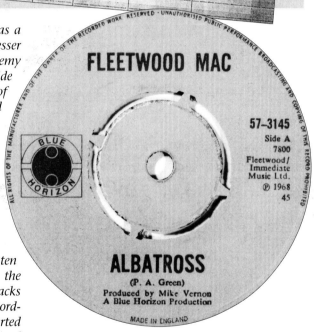

ARTIST FLEETWOOD MAC CHICKEN SHACK * TITLE	DATE 9 OCT	SINGLE	E.P.	L.P.	MONO STEREO ✓	JOB No.	PRODUCER MIKE VERNON ENGINEER MIKE ROSS
	TAPE No.	TAKE No.	MATRIX No.		DURATION		COMMENT
ONE SUNNY DAY		T4					
THE ALBATROSS		T7			3.05		2ND STAGE MASTER
"LOVE THAT WOMAN"		T7					2ND STAGE MASTER
CRAZY FOR MY BABY		T7	← DO NOT USE				2ND STAGE MASTER
"LOVE THAT WOMAN"		T7					2ND STAGE MASTER
GOING MY WAY		T6					2ND STAGE MASTER
							2ND STAGE MASTER
"ID RATHER GO BLIND" *		T8	NEW RECORDING				2ND STAGE MASTER

MIKE VERNON: *It was a one-off. I guess it was a creation that Peter, John, Mick and to a lesser extent Danny had been working on. Jeremy wasn't involved in it at all. The floating slide guitar was Peter's, not Jeremy's, and like most of the Blue Horizon recordings, it was recorded with Mike Ross engineering. 'Albatross' was a departure from what the band had been doing but in a way it pre-empted what they were going to do, because 'Man Of The World' was just as much of a departure. I personally liked it but then I was a great fan of Santo & Johnny's 'Sleepwalk' and 'Albatross' was not dissimilar in some respects.*

MIKE ROSS: *We began recording 'Albatross' at ten in the morning and 'Jigsaw Puzzle Blues' in the afternoon and by 11 in the evening both tracks were mixed. Up until this point we always recorded the band live but with 'Albatross' we started with Mick playing tom-toms, which were mixed on the left and right channels, John on bass, and Danny and Peter on guitars. We overdubbed another guitar and cymbals after the basic track was laid down.*

This beautiful instrumental topped the British charts following its use by the BBC as a television theme although many blues purists who had followed the band since the groups inception were heard to cry 'Sellout!'

top *Paperwork from the overdub session for 'Albatross' and other titles.*

above *The label of the single release of 'Albatross'.*

ARTIST FLEETWOOD MAC	DATE	SINGLE	E.P.	L.P.	MONO		JOB No.	PRODUCER MIKE VERNON
TITLE	6 OCT			✓	STEREO	✓		ENGINEER MIKE ROSS
	TAPE No.		TAKE No.		MATRIX No.		DURATION	COMMENT
"ONE SUNNY DAY" X								
			T.1					
			T.2					NO
			T.3					OK
"SOMETHING INSIDE OF ME" X (check)							3.05	1ST STAGE MASTER
			T.1					
			T.2		Master			GOOD
"NEED YOUR LOVE SO BAD"			T.3					NO
U.S.A. VERSION X								NO
			T.1		←	DO NOT USE		

STUDIO SESSION FOR BLUE HORIZON
6 October 1968
CBS Studios, New Bond Street, London

One Sunny Day (Take 3)	ENGLISH ROSE
Something Inside Of Me (Take 1)	ENGLISH ROSE
Without You	ENGLISH ROSE
Need Your Love So Bad	Possible A-Side (US)

Vocal/Guitar/Harmonica: Peter Green
Guitar: Jeremy Spencer
Guitar: Danny Kirwan
Bass: John McVie
Drums: Mick Fleetwood

Producer: Mike Vernon
Engineer: Mike Ross

The version of 'Need Your Love So Bad' shown here as a US A-side may only be a different mix of the original recording from 28 April session. The tape box from this session definitely states USA Version but also states *Do Not Use*.

As MR WONDERFUL had not seen a release in the US a mixture of old and new material was assembled and released under the title ENGLISH ROSE to cash in on the groups recent US tour. The album featured nearly all the groups previous singles along with tracks lifted from MR WONDERFUL and a handful of new songs by Danny Kirwan that were originally intended for a future project. Once again the cover was designed to shock, this time a picture of Mick Fleetwood in drag!

top left *Tape box from 6 October. Note the USA version of* 'Need Your Love So Bad' *is marked 'Do Not Use'.*

bottom left *Publicity photo: (left to right) Mick Fleetwood, Peter Green, Jeremy Spencer, Danny Kirwan and John McVie.*

SESSION FOR 'RADIO 1 CLUB'
9 October 1968
Playhouse Theatre, London

Like Crying	Radio Broadcast/ LIVE AT THE BBC
Albatross	Radio Broadcast/ LIVE AT THE BBC
Hang Onto A Dream	Radio Broadcast/ LIVE AT THE BBC
Baby Don't You Want To Go	Radio Broadcast

Vocal/Guitar/Harmonica: Peter Green
Guitar: Jeremy Spencer
Guitar: Danny Kirwan
Bass: John McVie
Drums: Mick Fleetwood

Producer: —
Engineer: —

Broadcast on 5 November 1968

SESSION FOR BBC WORLD SERVICE 'RHYTHM & BLUES 26'
1 November 1968
Aeolian Hall, Studio 1, London

Hard-Headed Woman	Radio Broadcast
Sweet Home Chicago	Radio Broadcast/ LIVE AT THE BBC
Crazy About My Baby	Radio Broadcast
Baby Please Set A Date	Radio Broadcast

Vocal/Guitar/Harmonica: Peter Green
Guitar: Jeremy Spencer
Guitar: Danny Kirwan
Bass: John McVie
Drums: Mick Fleetwood
Keyboards: Christine Perfect

Producer: Jeff Griffin
Engineer: Joe Young

Broadcast on 26 November 1968

Peter Green's
Fleetwood Mac

the early years
1967 - 1970

15 Track VIDEO COLLECTION
Including
Albatross, Black Magic Woman, Oh Well,
Green Manalishi & Man of the World

Video cover from the 1996 release that featured many early clips of Fleetwood Mac.

THEN PLAY ON
1969–1973

MIKE VERNON had considered the idea of the band recording with some of Americas leading blues-men and, although he didn't have any real plans, his belief was that it would produce some fine music and also be fun. During their second US tour the opportunity arose to fulfill his plans. An associate of Vernons, Seymour Stein, put him in touch with Marshall Chess, owner of the famed Chess Studios. Founded in the early fifties by Phil and Leonard Chess the studios could boast an impressive roster of blues artists including Muddy Waters, Elmore James and John Lee Hooker and with the advent of rock 'n' roll the names Chuck Berry and Bo Diddely were added to the list. Willie Dixon put together the star names for the session and even though several were unavailable he made a good choice.

MIKE VERNON: *Thankfully, everyone who was supposed to turn up did. Marshall Chess and I took charge of affairs and left engineer Stu Black to take care of the sounds. I figured if he couldn't get a sound at Ter-Mar then nobody could. After all he had recorded everyone from Muddy to Sonny Boy . . . There was no real sense of urgency. When everyone had decided what to record next we just got on with it. In Jeremy's case it was easy – he picked a bunch of his favourite Elmore James songs that he had not already recorded and let rip.*

One of the highlights from the session was Jeremy Spencer's rendition of Elmore James' 'Madison Blues' on which he was accompanied by J T Brown, James' saxophone player from the fifties.

STUDIO SESSION FOR BLUE HORIZON
4 January 1969
Ter-Mar Studios, Chicago

Reel # 1

Watch Out [1]	BLUES JAM AT CHESS
Ooh Baby [2]	BLUES JAM AT CHESS
South Indiana # 1 [3]	BLUES JAM AT CHESS
Last Night [4]	BLUES JAM AT CHESS
South Indiana # 2 [3]	BLUES JAM AT CHESS
Red Hot Jam [5]	BLUES JAM AT CHESS
I Need Your Love [7]	BLUES JAM AT CHESS
Horton's Boogie Woogie	*Unissued*

Reel # 2

Instrumental	*Unissued*
Instrumental	*Unissued*
I'm Worried [6]	BLUES JAM AT CHESS
I Held My Baby Last Night [6]	BLUES JAM AT CHESS
Madison Blues [6]	BLUES JAM AT CHESS
I Can't Hold Out [6]	BLUES JAM AT CHESS
Bobby's Blues	*Unissued*
I Need Your Love	*Unissued*
Instrumental (uptempo)	*Unissued*
Instrumental	*Unissued*
Have A Good Time	*Unissued*
Instrumental (uptempo)	*Unissued*

Reel Numbers Unknown

Rockin' Boogie [12]	BLUES JAM AT CHESS
World's In A Tangle [8]	BLUES JAM AT CHESS
Talk With You [9]	BLUES JAM AT CHESS
Like It This Way [9]	BLUES JAM AT CHESS
Sugar Mama [13]	BLUES JAM AT CHESS
Homework [13]	BLUES JAM AT CHESS
Ain't Nobody's Business	*Unissued*
Someday Soon Baby [10]	BLUES JAM AT CHESS
I Got The Blues [7]	BLUES JAM AT CHESS
Have A Good Time	*Unissued*
Rock Me Baby	*Unissued*

Reel # 5

Hungry Country Girl [10]	BLUES JAM AT CHESS
Black Jack Blues [11]	BLUES JAM AT CHESS
Everyday I Have The Blues [12]	BLUES JAM AT CHESS
Instrumental	*Unissued*
My Baby's Gone	THE BLUE HORIZON STORY 1965–1970 (VOLUME 1)

1 Vocal/Guitar: Peter Green
Guitar: Danny Kirwan
Bass: John McVie
Drums: Mick Fleetwood

2 Vocal/Guitar: Peter Green
Bass: John McVie
Drums: Mick Fleetwood

3 Guitar: Peter Green
Guitar: Danny Kirwan
Bass: John McVie
Drums: Mick Fleetwood
Harmonica: Walter 'Shakey' Horton

4 Vocal/Guitar: Peter Green
Harmonica: Walter 'Shakey' Horton
Guitar: Danny Kirwan
Bass: John McVie
Drums: Mick Fleetwood

5 Guitar: Peter Green
Harmonica: Walter 'Shakey' Horton
Guitar: 'Guitar' Buddy
Guitar: Honey Boy Edwards
String Bass: Willie Dixon
Drums: Mick Fleetwood

6 Vocal/Slide Guitar: Jeremy Spencer
Tenor Sax: J T Brown
Guitar: Danny Kirwan
String Bass: Willie Dixon
Drums: Mick Fleetwood

7 Vocal/Harmonica: Walter 'Shakey' Horton
Guitar: Peter Green
Guitar: Danny Kirwan
Piano: Otis Spann
Bass: John McVie
Drums: S P Leary

8 Vocal/Guitar: Danny Kirwan
Guitar: Peter Green
Piano: Otis Spann
Bass: John McVie
Drums: S P Leary

9 Vocal/Guitar: Danny Kirwan
Guitar: Peter Green
Piano: Otis Spann
Bass: John McVie
Drums: S P Leary

10 Vocal/Piano: Otis Spann
Guitar: Peter Green
Guitar: Danny Kirwan
Bass: John McVie
Drums: Mick Fleetwood

11 Vocal/Tenor Sax: J T Brown
Guitar: Jeremy Spencer
Guitar: Honey Boy Edwards
String Bass: Willie Dixon
Drums: Mick Fleetwood

12 Vocal/Slide Guitar: Jeremy Spencer
Tenor Sax: J T Brown
Guitar: Peter Green
Guitar: Honey Boy Edwards
String Bass: Willie Dixon
Drums: Mick Fleetwood

13 Vocal/Guitar: Peter Green
Guitar: Danny Kirwan
Piano: Otis Spann
Bass: John McVie
Drums: Mick Fleetwood

Producer: Mike Vernon/Marshall Chess
Engineer: Stu Black

Tape box covers from the historic
'Chess' sessions detailing the many
unissued titles.

Paperwork from this historic session show several unissued items, and although we can give details on some of the original session reels many were not available, leaving details of the unissued instrumentals vague. Many of these could have been early run-throughs of material they recorded later.

It would be a year before Blue Horizon would release the material on a double album entitled BLUES JAM AT CHESS. The album included alternate takes, studio chat from the musicians and engineers instructions.

Fleetwood Mac's next task was as house band on Otis Spann's album THE BIGGEST THING SINCE COLOSSUS.

Otis Spann was born in a small farming community in the Delta State of Mississippi on 21 March 1930 and received his early tuition from a local blues pianist called Friday Ford. In the late forties, like many other locals, he moved north and settled in Chicago. At the same time as Spann's move another local blues musician headed north. McKinley Morganfield (Muddy Waters) employed Spann as his guitarist and he remained for many years. Throughout the fifties and early sixties he worked on many fine albums and in January 1969 found himself at Tempo Sound Studios in New York City with Fleetwood Mac.

Documentation from the 'Chess' sessions, 1969.

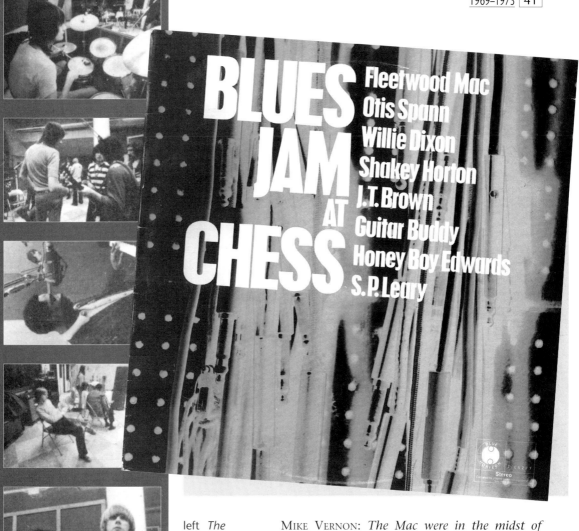

BLUES JAM AT CHESS

Fleetwood Mac
Otis Spann
Willie Dixon
Shakey Horton
J. T. Brown
Guitar Buddy
Honey Boy Edwards
S. P. Leary

Stereo

left *The Mac at work. Photos from the 'Chess' sessions.*

above *The original album cover artwork.*

MIKE VERNON: *The Mac were in the midst of their second US tour and several days recording had already been arranged at the Ter-Mar Studios in Chicago from which the* BLUES JAM AT CHESS *package was subsequently taken. One of the artists involved in that project was Otis Spann and the relationship that was built up even over such a short space of time led to my belief that a solo album featuring both acts would make for some great listening. The only difficult decision that had to be taken was in relation to the drummer. Otis was used to working with long-time associate S P Leary and he felt happier in his mind at having that personal bond with at least one of the sidemen on the recording date. Mick Fleetwood very graciously stepped down and let the flamboyant S P onto the drum stool.*

STUDIO SESSION FOR BLUE HORIZON
9 January 1969
Tempo Sound Studios, New York

My Love Depends On You	THE BIGGEST THING SINCE COLOSSUS
Walkin'	A-side/THE BIGGEST THING SINCE COLOSSUS
It Was A Big Thing	THE BIGGEST THING SINCE COLOSSUS
Temperature Is Rising (98.8°F)	B-side
Temperature Is Rising (100.2°F)	THE BIGGEST THING SINCE COLOSSUS
Dig You	THE BIGGEST THING SINCE COLOSSUS
No More Doggin'	THE BIGGEST THING SINCE COLOSSUS
Ain't Nobody's Business	THE BIGGEST THING SINCE COLOSSUS
She Needs Some Loving	THE BIGGEST THING SINCE COLOSSUS
I Need Some Air	THE BIGGEST THING SINCE COLOSSUS
Someday Baby	THE BIGGEST THING SINCE COLOSSUS
Blues For Hippies	BLUES FOR HIPPIES

Vocal/Piano: Otis Spann
Guitar/Harmonica: Peter Green
Guitar: Danny Kirwan
Bass: John McVie
Drums: S P Leary

Producer: Mike Vernon
Engineer: Warren Slaten

MIKE VERNON: *In my own personal estimation, Peter Green was just the very best blues guitarist this country has ever produced, and if anybody wants any proof of that all they have to do is listen to the Otis Spann album I did with Fleetwood Mac,* THE BIGGEST THING SINCE COLOSSUS. *Some of the guitar playing on that is absolutely stunning and it's all from the heart.*

Cover of the CD release THE BIGGEST THING SINCE COLOSSUS *on which Fleetwood Mac were the session musicians.*

STUDIO SESSION FOR BLUE HORIZON
10–12 January 1969
Tempo Sound, New York

Man Of The World	A-side

Vocal/Guitar/Harmonica: Peter Green
Guitar: Jeremy Spencer
Guitar: Danny Kirwan
Bass: John McVie
Drums: Mick Fleetwood

Producer: Mike Vernon/Fleetwood Mac
Engineer:

Although recorded for Blue Horizon this track was released on Andrew Loog Oldham's Immediate label as the group's contract with Blue Horizon had expired. Throughout the coming months the group searched for another label and were, at one point, considering going with the Beatle's new label, Apple, but in the end signed with Warner's Reprise label.

STUDIO SESSION FOR IMMEDIATE
Early 1969
Recorded Sound, London

Somebody's Gonna Get Their Head Kicked In Tonight	B-side

Vocal/Guitar/Harmonica: Peter Green
Guitar: Jeremy Spencer
Guitar: Danny Kirwan
Bass: John McVie
Drums: Mick Fleetwood

Producer: Mike Vernon/Fleetwood Mac
Engineer:

'Somebody's Gonna Get Their Head Kicked In Tonight' was credited to Earl Vince and the Valiants and was the first released example of Jeremy Spencer's love of fifties rock 'n' roll.

SESSION FOR RADIO 1 'TOP GEAR'
10 March 1969
Playhouse Theatre, London

You'll Never Know What You're Missing Till You Try	Radio Broadcast/ LIVE AT THE BBC
Blues With A Feeling	Radio Broadcast/ LIVE AT THE BBC
Heavenly	Radio Broadcast/ LIVE AT THE BBC
I Can't Believe You Want To Leave	Radio Broadcast/ LIVE AT THE BBC
Tallahassie Lassie *	Radio Broadcast/ LIVE AT THE BBC
Early Morning Come *	Radio Broadcast/ LIVE AT THE BBC

Vocal/Guitar/Harmonica: Peter Green
Guitar: Jeremy Spencer
Guitar: Danny Kirwan
Bass: John McVie
Drums: Mick Fleetwood

Producer: Bernie Andrews
Engineer: Pete Ritzema

Broadcast on 16 March 1969 (except * broadcast 11 May 1969)

SESSION FOR RADIO 1 'SYMONDS ON SUNDAY'
17 March 1969
Aeolian Hall, Studio 2, London

You'll Be Mine	Radio Broadcast
Roll Along Blues	Radio Broadcast
Peggy Sue Got Married	Radio Broadcast
Albatross	Radio Broadcast
Shady Little Baby *	Radio Broadcast
Hot Rodding *	Radio Broadcast
New Worried Blues *	Radio Broadcast

Vocal/Guitar/Harmonica: Peter Green
Guitar: Jeremy Spencer
Guitar: Danny Kirwan
Bass: John McVie
Drums: Mick Fleetwood
Keyboards: Christine Perfect

Guitar: Alexis Korner *
Harmonica: Duster Bennett *

Producer: John Walters
Engineer: Tony Wilson

Broadcast on 23 March 1969

LIVE RECORDING
April 1969
Amsterdam

Merry Go Round	ROUGHAGE '69
One Sided Love	ROUGHAGE '69
Dust My Broom	ROUGHAGE '69
Got To Move	ROUGHAGE '69
Sugar Mama	ROUGHAGE '69
Can't Hold Out	ROUGHAGE '69
Stop Messin' Round	ROUGHAGE '69
San Ho Zay	ROUGHAGE '69
Albatross	ROUGHAGE '69
Blue Suede Shoes	ROUGHAGE '69

Vocal/Guitar/Harmonica: Peter Green
Guitar: Jeremy Spencer
Guitar: Danny Kirwan
Bass: John McVie
Drums: Mick Fleetwood

Producer: —
Engineer: —

STUDIO SESSION FOR REPRISE
April–July 1969
Studio Unknown

Coming Your Way	B-side (US)/THEN PLAY ON
Fighting For Madge	THEN PLAY ON
When You Say	THEN PLAY ON
Show-Biz Blues	THEN PLAY ON
Under Way	THEN PLAY ON
Although The Sun Is Shining	THEN PLAY ON
Rattlesnake Shake	A-side(US)/ THEN PLAY ON
Searching For Madge	THEN PLAY ON
My Dream	THEN PLAY ON
Like Crying	THEN PLAY ON
Before The Beginning	THEN PLAY ON

Oh Well (Part 1)	A-side/THEN PLAY ON
Oh Well (Part 2)	B-side/THEN PLAY ON
Close My Eyes	

Vocal/Guitar/Harmonica: Peter Green
Guitar: Danny Kirwan
Bass: John McVie
Drums: Mick Fleetwood
Vocal/Keyboards: Christine McVie

Producer: Fleetwood Mac
Engineer: Martin Birch

MICK FLEETWOOD: *Peter Green was responsible for forming Fleetwood Mac, which was very much a blues band, but 'Oh Well' demonstrates how strong a songwriter he was. We did the track around the time we did* THEN PLAY ON, *but it didn't go on the album at first, though they put it on later.*
(Record Hunter, February 1992)

Jeremy Spencer did not appear on THEN PLAY ON feeling he had nothing to offer and although the album was due to be released with a bonus extended-play featuring Jeremy's rock 'n' roll parodies the idea was scrapped at the last moment.

SESSION FOR WORLD SERVICE
'RHYTHM & BLUES'
14 May 1969
Maida Vale 4, London

All Over Again	Radio Broadcast
Talk With You	Radio Broadcast
Just Want To Tell You	Radio Broadcast

Vocal/Guitar/Harmonica: Peter Green
Guitar: Jeremy Spencer
Guitar: Danny Kirwan
Bass: John McVie
Drums: Mick Fleetwood

Producer: Jeff Griffin
Engineer: Joe Young

Broadcast on 2 June 1969

SESSION FOR 'CHRIS GRANT'S TASTY POP SUNDAE'
10 June 1969
201 Piccadilly, Studio 1, London

Coming Your Way	Radio Broadcast
Man Of The World	Radio Broadcast/ LIVE AT THE BBC
Jumping At Shadows	Radio Broadcast/ LIVE AT THE BBC
Linda	Radio Broadcast/ LIVE AT THE BBC

Vocal/Guitar/Harmonica: Peter Green
Guitar: Jeremy Spencer
Guitar: Danny Kirwan
Bass: John McVie
Drums: Mick Fleetwood
Keyboards: Christine Perfect

Producer: Paul Williams
Engineer: —

Broadcast on 15 June 1969

SESSION FOR RADIO 1 'DLT'
6 October 1969
Aeolian Hall, Studio 2, London

Linda	Radio Broadcast
Oh Well (Part 1)	Radio Broadcast/ Live At The BBC
Although The Sun Is Shining	Radio Broadcast/ Live At The BBC

Vocal/Guitar/Harmonica: Peter Green
Guitar: Jeremy Spencer
Guitar: Danny Kirwan
Bass: John McVie
Drums: Mick Fleetwood

Producer: Paul Williams
Engineer: —

Broadcast on 12 October 1969

BOB BRUNNING: *In spite of Fleetwood Mac's astonishingly hectic schedule during 1969, members were kind enough to come and contribute to two albums I recorded during that year. Peter Green played magnificently on my Brunning Sunflower Blues Band album* TRACKSIDE BLUES *and Mick Fleetwood and Danny Kirwan joined Bob Hall and myself on our first* TRAMP *album*

STUDIO SESSION FOR REPRISE
Early 1970 – Exact Date Unknown
Studio Unknown

World In Harmony	B-side

Vocal/Guitar/Harmonica: Peter Green
Guitar: Jeremy Spencer
Guitar: Danny Kirwan
Bass: John McVie
Drums: Mick Fleetwood
Vocal/Keyboards: Christine McVie

Producer: Fleetwood Mac
Engineer: Martin Birch

During their third tour of the US, Fleetwood Mac appeared at a series of shows that became known as The Boston Tea Party.

LIVE RECORDINGS
5–7 February 1970
Boston

Oh Well (Part 1)	LIVE IN BOSTON/ CERULEAN/MADISON BLUES
Like It This Way	LIVE IN BOSTON/ CERULEAN/MADISON BLUES
World In Harmony	LIVE IN BOSTON/ CERULEAN/MADISON BLUES
Only You	LIVE IN BOSTON/ CERULEAN/MADISON BLUES
Black Magic Woman	LIVE IN BOSTON/ CERULEAN/MADISON BLUES
Jumping At Shadows	LIVE IN BOSTON/ CERULEAN
Can't Hold On	LIVE IN BOSTON/ CERULEAN/MADISON BLUES

Sandy Mary	CERULEAN/MADISON BLUES
Stranger Blues	CERULEAN
Great Balls Of Fire	CERULEAN
Jenny, Jenny	CERULEAN
Oh Baby	CERULEAN
Teenage Darling	CERULEAN/MADISON BLUES
Loving Kind	CERULEAN
Keep-A-Knocking	CERULEAN
Red Hot Mama	CERULEAN/MADISON BLUES
Tutti Frutti	CERULEAN
Madison Blues	CERULEAN/MADISON BLUES
Got To Move	CERULEAN/MADISON BLUES
Green Manalishi	CERULEAN/MADISON BLUES
Rattlesnake Shake	CERULEAN

Vocal/Guitar: Peter Green
Guitar: Jeremy Spencer
Guitar: Danny Kirwan
Bass: John McVie
Drums: Mick Fleetwood

Producer:—
Engineer: —

There were plans to release an album featuring some of the material performed at The Boston Tea Party shows but the idea was dropped, possibly due to Peter Green's sudden departure from the group. However, this material has been made available on numerous unofficial releases, most notably, CERULEAN which featured the complete sixteen-minute version of 'Green Manalishi' and the nearly twenty-five-minute-long 'Rattlesnake Shake'. The album also featured part of the set that the group performed as Earl Vince and The Valiants, Spencer's pastiche of 1950s rock 'n' roll. Other releases contained selected highlights from the shows.

**SESSION FOR RADIO 1 'IN CONCERT –
FEATURING FLEETWOOD MAC'
9 April 1970
Paris Cinema, Lower Regent Street,
London**

Rattlesnake Shake	Radio Broadcast/ LIVE AT THE BBC/ MERELY A PORTMANTEAU

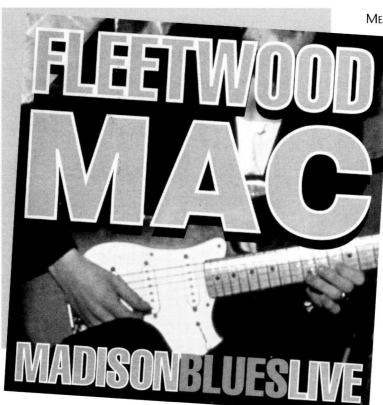

One of many releases to feature material from The Boston Tea Party tapes recorded in February 1970.

Under Way	Radio Broadcast/
	MERELY A PORTMANTEAU
Tiger	Radio Broadcast/
	MERELY A PORTMANTEAU
Green Manalishi	Radio Broadcast/
	MERELY A PORTMANTEAU
Stranger Blues	Radio Broadcast/
	MERELY A PORTMANTEAU
World In Harmony	Radio Broadcast/
	MERELY A PORTMANTEAU
Great Balls Of Fire	Radio Broadcast/
	MERELY A PORTMANTEAU
Twist And Shout	Radio Broadcast/
	MERELY A PORTMANTEAU

Vocal/Guitar/Harmonica: Peter Green
Guitar: Jeremy Spencer
Guitar: Danny Kirwan
Bass: John McVie
Drums: Mick Fleetwood

Producer: —
Engineer: —

Broadcast on 19 April 1970

SESSION FOR RADIO 1 'TOP GEAR'
27 April 1970
Playhouse Theatre, London

Sandy Mary	Radio Broadcast/
	LIVE AT THE BBC
World In Harmony	Radio Broadcast
Tiger	Radio Broadcast
Only You	Radio Broadcast/
	LIVE AT THE BBC
Leaving Town Blues	Radio Broadcast

Vocal/Guitar/Harmonica: Peter Green
Guitar: Jeremy Spencer
Guitar: Danny Kirwan
Bass: John McVie
Drums: Mick Fleetwood
Violin: Nick Pickett

Producer: John Walters
Engineer: Tony Wilson

Broadcast on 23 May 1970

STUDIO SESSION FOR REPRISE
April 1970
Warner-Reprise Studios, Los Angeles

Green Manalishi	A-side

Vocal/Guitar/Harmonica: Peter Green
Guitar: Jeremy Spencer
Guitar: Danny Kirwan
Bass: John McVie
Drums: Mick Fleetwood
Vocal/Keyboards: Christine McVie

Producer: Fleetwood Mac
Engineer: Martin Birch

MARTIN BIRCH: *The weirdest session I've ever taken part in. Peter wasn't communicating very much and Jeremy was well into his Children Of God thing. The whole atmosphere was very, very strange.*

PETER GREEN: *Making 'Green Manalishi' was one of the best memories. Mixing it down in the studio and listening back to it, I thought it would make number one: lots of drums, bass guitars, all kinds of things, double-up on bass guitars, six string basses, tracking on it. Danny Kirwan and me playing those shrieking guitars together.*

It was in April that Peter Green announced he was leaving Fleetwood Mac. The band reeled at this announcement and had to cancel their forthcoming tour dates. Problems had started back in 1969 when Green had the idea that the band should give away all their money. This idea, obviously, met with little enthusiasm from other band members. A tour of Europe in early 1970 created the next problem. Green had got involved with a group of German hippies, the 'Munich Jet Set' as the band called them, and was invited to a party where he took what turned out to be impure LSD. Tragically it would have serious effects on Green.

JOHN McVIE: *In Spring 1970, Peter Green, who'd been thinking about leaving for some time,*

suddenly said 'enough is enough'. It was in Munich – right in the middle of a European tour – but he worked out all the contracted gigs, and left six weeks later. He just didn't want to be a guitar star anymore . . . all the pressures, possibly coupled with a degree of acid loss, seemed to put him off the rock scene. At the time he left, he was getting into free-form playing, spacing out – and I think his solo album was probably a reflection of the state of his mind that summer.
(The Complete Rock Family Trees)

BOB BRUNNING: *I was very worried about Peter around that time. He and I had worked together on Dave Kelly's 1970 solo album on Mercury, and I invited him round to my house to listen to it. But he refused to listen to the record, saying he had no interest in music and suggested we went to the pub instead. This was the man who had frowned upon me drinking more than one pint during evening rehearsals! This was certainly not the Peter I knew.*

CHRISTINE MCVIE: *John and the band were working up a new album and a new stage act following Peter Green's departure that May. They were down to a four-piece, and just before the start of a tour, they suddenly felt they needed another instrument to fill out the sound . . . and there I was – sitting around doing next to nothing and knowing all the songs back to front because I'd been watching them rehearsing for the past three months.*
(The Complete Rock Family Trees)

The band were living in a converted oast barn in the Hampshire countryside and it was to there that the band retired, following Green's departure, to start work on their next album.

STUDIO SESSION FOR REPRISE
June–July 1970
Kiln House, Hampshire

This Is The Rock	KILN HOUSE
Station Man	B-side (US)/KILN HOUSE
Blood On The Floor	KILN HOUSE
Hi Ho Silver	KILN HOUSE
Jewel Eyed Judy	A-side (US)/KILN HOUSE
Buddy's Song	KILN HOUSE

Earl Gray	KILN HOUSE
One Together	KILN HOUSE
Tell Me All The Things You Do	KILN HOUSE
Mission Bell	KILN HOUSE

Guitar/Vocal/Piano: Jeremy Spencer
Guitar/Vocal: Danny Kirwan
Bass: John McVie
Drums: Mick Fleetwood
Vocal/Keyboards: Christine McVie

Producer: Fleetwood Mac
Engineer: Martin Birch

This was the first album without Peter Green and it had a heavy American fifties influence with the inclusion of the rockabilly 'This Is The Rock', Holly-influenced 'Buddy's Song' and the countryfied 'Blood On The Floor'. It is interesting to note that before Green's departure the follow up to THEN PLAY ON was to be called 'Sandy Mary'.

SESSION FOR BBC RADIO 'FIRST GEAR'
7 July 1970
Maida Vale 4, London

Buddy's Song	Radio Broadcast/ LIVE AT THE BBC
When Will I Be Loved	Radio Broadcast/ LIVE AT THE BBC
Jenny Lee	Radio Broadcast/ LIVE AT THE BBC
When I See My Baby	Radio Broadcast/ LIVE AT THE BBC
Honey Hush	Radio Broadcast/ LIVE AT THE BBC

Guitar: Jeremy Spencer
Guitar: Danny Kirwan
Bass: John McVie
Drums: Mick Fleetwood

Producer: John Walters
Engineer: Bob Conduct

Broadcast on 22 July 1970

SESSION FOR BBC 'RADIO 1 CLUB'
10 November 1970
Paris Cinema, Lower Regent Street,
London

Sandy Mary	Radio Broadcast
Crazy About You Baby	Radio Broadcast
Down At The Crown For Now	Radio Broadcast
Turn Me Loose *	Radio Broadcast
Tell Me All The Things You Do	Radio Broadcast

Guitar: Jeremy Spencer
Guitar: Danny Kirwan
Bass: John McVie

Drums: Mick Fleetwood
Keyboards/Vocals: Christine Perfect

Producer: —
Engineer: —

Broadcast on 14 December 1970 (except *
broadcast 16 December 1970)

STUDIO SESSION FOR REPRISE
Late 1970
Studio Unknown

Dragonfly	A-side
Purple Dancer	B-side

Guitar: Jeremy Spencer
Guitar: Danny Kirwan
Bass: John McVie
Drums: Mick Fleetwood
Vocal/Keyboards: Christine McVie

Fleetwood Mac pose for a photo with new member Christine McVie.

Producer: Fleetwood Mac
Engineer: Martin Birch

SESSION FOR BBC RADIO 'MIKE HARDING – SOUND OF THE SEVENTIES'
24 November 1970
Maida Vale 5, London

Down At The Crown For Now	Radio Broadcast
Purple Dancer	Radio Broadcast
Station Man	Radio Broadcast

Guitar: Jeremy Spencer
Guitar: Danny Kirwan
Bass: John McVie
Drums: Mick Fleetwood
Keyboards/Vocals: Christine McVie

Producer: Malcolm Brown
Engineer: Mike Harding/Mike Franks

Broadcast on 1 December 1970

SESSION FOR BBC RADIO
5 January 1971
Maida Vale 4, London

Start Again	Radio Broadcast
Teenage Darling	Radio Broadcast
Preachin'	Radio Broadcast/ LIVE AT THE BBC
Get Like You Used To Be	Radio Broadcast
Dragonfly *	Radio Broadcast

Guitar: Jeremy Spencer
Guitar: Danny Kirwan
Bass: John McVie
Drums: Mick Fleetwood
Keyboards/Vocals: Christine Perfect

Producer: —
Engineer: Bob Conduct

Broadcast on 23 January 1971 (except * broadcast 27 March 1971)

In February 1971, halfway through a successful American tour, Jeremy Spencer went missing. Eventually he was tracked down to a religious colony *The Children Of God*. He had started having doubts about his fame and fortune, not unlike Peter Green months earlier, and felt he could no longer carry on in the band. Although Mick Fleetwood tried to talk to him he accepted Spencer's decision. It would be a long time before any of the group would see him again.

JOHN MCVIE: *I was sitting next to him on the plane down from San Fransisco to Los Angeles where we had some gigs at the Whiskey A Go Go. He was looking out of the window, and then he suddenly turned to me and said 'Why do I have to be here if I really don't want to be here?' Well, everyone in the band had felt like that at one time or another so I didn't give it a second thought . . . but that was the last time I spoke to him for two years.*
(The Complete Rock Family Trees)

To enable them to complete their American tour they called on Peter Green who agreed to fly out and play the remaining dates.

On their return to Britain they began working on their next album with a new member. The American, Bob Welch, was introduced to the group by Judy Wong and, along with Christine McVie, he wrote all the songs for what would become FUTURE GAMES, their next album release.

MICK FLEETWOOD: *Bob was a major player. When we first went to America he helped us become a healthy underground band that not only had an audience but could also sell 250,000 albums every release.*
(Record Hunter, February 1992)

BOB WELCH: *I had some songs that fit and they liked them enough to put them on the album. There was no producer; it was up to mutual consensus among Fleetwood Mac to make the decisions.*
(Fleetwood: My Life And Adventures In Fleetwood Mac)

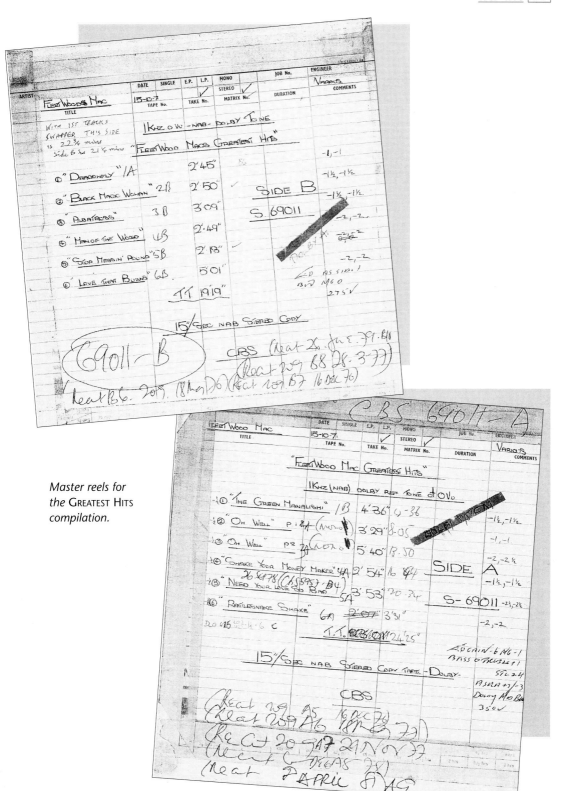

*Master reels for
the* GREATEST HITS
compilation.

STUDIO SESSION FOR REPRISE
June–August 1971
Advision Studios, London

Woman Of A 1000 Years	FUTURE GAMES
Morning Rain	FUTURE GAMES
What A Shame	FUTURE GAMES
Future Games	FUTURE GAMES
Sands Of Time	A-side (US)/
	FUTURE GAMES
Sometimes	FUTURE GAMES
Lay It All Down	B-side (US)/
	FUTURE GAMES
Lay It All Down	25 YEARS – THE CHAIN
(alternate version)	
Show Me A Smile	FUTURE GAMES

Guitar/Vocals: Bob Welch
Guitar/Vocals: Danny Kirwan
Bass: John McVie
Drums: Mick Fleetwood
Keyboards/Vocals: Christine Perfect
Saxophones: John Perfect

Producer: Fleetwood Mac
Engineer: Martin Rushent

SESSION FOR BBC RADIO 'ALAN BLACK – SOUND OF THE SEVENTIES'
1 July 1971
Aeolian Hall, Studio 2, London

Woman Of A Thousand Years	Radio Broadcast
Show Me A Smile	Radio Broadcast
Future Games	Radio Broadcast

Guitar: Bob Welch
Guitar: Danny Kirwan
Bass: John McVie
Drums: Mick Fleetwood
Keyboards/Vocals: Christine Perfect

Producer: John Muir
Engineer: John White

Broadcast on 23 July 1971

Fleetwood Mac spent most of 1972 touring Europe and America. During a week's break they returned to London and recorded their next album. On their return to America the tapes were damaged when going through the x-ray at the airport and work had to be done at a studio in New York to repair them.

STUDIO SESSION FOR REPRISE
Early 1972
DeLane Lea Music Centre, London

Child Of Mine	BARE TREES
The Ghost	BARE TREES
Homeward Bound	BARE TREES
Sunny Side Of Heaven	B-side (US)/
	BARE TREES
Bare Trees	BARE TREES
Sentimental Lady	A-side (US)/
	BARE TREES
Danny's Chant	BARE TREES
Spare Me A Little Of Your Love	A-side (US)/
	BARE TREES
Dust	BARE TREES
Thoughts On A Grey Day	BARE TREES
Trinity	25 YEARS – THE CHAIN

Guitar/Vocal/Piano: Bob Welch
Guitar/Vocal: Danny Kirwan
Bass: John McVie
Drums: Mick Fleetwood
Vocal/Keyboards: Christine McVie

Producer: Fleetwood Mac
Engineer: Martin Birch

The Fleetwood Mac curse was about to hit another guitarist, this time Danny Kirwan. His behaviour had become strange and during a show on their 1972 tour he threw a fit in the dressing room, refused to go on stage and spent the show sitting at the mixing desk. After the show he proceeded to criticize the group and their performance. He was eventually sacked.

With another album to record Dave Walker was brought in as Kirwan's replacement.

Artwork from two early seventies albums – FUTURE GAMES and BARE TREES.

JOHN MCVIE: *We met Dave Walker on a tour we did with Savoy Brown; he was their singer. We thought we'd try having a front-man/vocalist which we'd never done before – but it only lasted about eight months.*
(The Complete Rock Family Trees)

Following the tour and Kirwan's departure Fleetwood Mac returned to the home they had brought back in 1970, a large house called Benifolds in Hampshire. It was there that they recorded their next album PENGUIN, using the famous Rolling Stones Mobile Studio.

JOHN MCVIE: *I used to live near London Zoo, and was an associate member of the Zoological Society; you paid an annual subscription and could go in free at any time. Well, I used to photograph animals, and the penguins in particular really fascinated me. . . I didn't sit there and talk to them or anything like that, but I used to spend hours just watching them and reading books about them. When the group decided to adopt a logo – some sort of visual symbol which people would associate with Fleetwood Mac – we decided that a penguin would be appropriate.*
(The Complete Rock Family Trees)

STUDIO SESSION FOR REPRISE
January–February 1973
Benifolds, Hampshire (Recorded by the Rolling Stones Mobile Unit)

Nightwatch	PENGUIN
Remember Me	A-side (US)/PENGUIN
Bright Fire	PENGUIN
Dissatisfied	B-side (US)/Penguin
(I'm A) Road Runner	PENGUIN
The Derelict	A-side/PENGUIN
Revelation	B-side (US)/PENGUIN
Did You Ever Love Me	A-side/PENGUIN
Caught In The Rain	PENGUIN

Lead Guitar/Slide Guitar: Bob Weston
Vocals: Dave Walker
Guitar: Bob Welch
Bass: John McVie
Drums: Mick Fleetwood
Vocal/Keyboards: Christine McVie
Organ: Steve Nye ('Night Watch' only)
Guitar: Peter Green ('Nightwatch' only)
Steel Drums: Ralph Richardson/Russel Valdez/
 Fred Totesaut ('Did You Ever Love Me' only)

Producer: Fleetwood Mac/Martin Birch
Engineer: Martin Birch

STUDIO SESSION FOR REPRISE
Summer 1973
Benifolds, Hampshire (Recorded by the Rolling Stones Mobile Unit)

Emerald Eyes	MYSTERY TO ME
Believe Me	MYSTERY TO ME
Just Crazy Love	MYSTERY TO ME
Hypnotized	B-side/MYSTERY TO ME
Forever	MYSTERY TO ME
Keep On Going	MYSTERY TO ME

PENGUIN was *the first album to feature what was to become the group's logo.*

In The City	MYSTERY TO ME
Miles Away	MYSTERY TO ME
Somebody	MYSTERY TO ME
The Way I Feel	MYSTERY TO ME
For Your Love	A-side/MYSTERY TO ME
Why	MYSTERY TO ME
Good Things	*Unissued*

Lead Guitar/Slide Guitar: Bob Weston
Vocals: Bob Welch
Bass: John McVie
Percussion: Mick Fleetwood
Keyboards/Vocals: Christine McVie
String Arrangements: Richard Hewson

Producers: Martin Birch/Fleetwood Mac
Engineer: Martin Birch
Assistant Engineers: Desmond Majekodunmi/
   Paul Hardiman

Session note: 'Good Things' was originally sched-uled to be on the album but a few weeks before release it was dropped and replaced with 'For Your Love'.

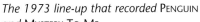

JOHN MCVIE: *We had co-opted Bob Weston from Long John Baldry's backing band. He was with us for just over a year and was asked to leave after a disagreement.*
(The Complete Rock Family Trees)

The 1973 line-up that recorded PENGUIN *and* MYSTERY TO ME.

FLEETWOOD MAC, *also known as the White Fleetwood Mac Album to distinguish it from their debut album, was the first to feature the talents of Stevie Nicks and Lindsey Buckingham.*

HEROES ARE HARD TO FIND
1974–1975

AFTER THE DEPARTURE of Bob Weston the band cancelled the rest of their US tour, and this was to bring about one of the strangest episodes in the history of Fleetwood Mac. Claiming that he owned the name Fleetwood Mac, Clifford Davis formed what has been known as the fake Fleetwood Mac and this was the band that toured America in early 1974. Legal wrangles followed which are all beyond the scope of this book and have been well covered in other publications. Suffice to say that the real Fleetwood Mac had to struggle to get recognized.

In July they recorded HEROES ARE HARD TO FIND. This was to be Bob Welch's last album with Fleetwood Mac, at Christmas he quit.

STUDIO SESSION FOR REPRISE
July 1974
Angel City Sound, Los Angeles

Heroes Are Hard To Find	A-side/ HEROES ARE HARD TO FIND
Coming Home	HEROES ARE HARD TO FIND
Angel	HEROES ARE HARD TO FIND
Bermuda Triangle	HEROES ARE HARD TO FIND
Come A Little Bit Closer	HEROES ARE HARD TO FIND
She's Changing Me	HEROES ARE HARD TO FIND
Bad Loser	HEROES ARE HARD TO FIND
Silver Heels	HEROES ARE HARD TO FIND
Prove Your Love	HEROES ARE HARD TO FIND
Born Enchanter	B-side/ HEROES ARE HARD TO FIND
Safe Harbour	HEROES ARE HARD TO FIND

Guitars/Vocals/Vibes: Bob Welch
Bass: John McVie
Drums/Percussion: Mick Fleetwood
Vocal/Keyboards/Arp String Ensemble: Christine McVie
Pedal Steel: Pete Kleinow ('Come A Little Bit Closer' only)

Producer: Fleetwood Mac/Bob Hughes
Engineers: Bob Hughes/Doug Graves

BOB BRUNNING: *Considering the traumas the Mac were going through in 1974, it was astonishingly kind of Mick Fleetwood and Danny Kirwan to find the time and energy to make a hugely energetic contribution to my second TRAMP album. They joined myself, Bob Hall, Jo-Anne and Dave Kelly in London for one day in the tiny Southern Music studio in London's Denmark Street for a rip-roaring session.*

LIVE RECORDINGS
December 1974
Los Angeles

Green Manalishi	BERMUDA TRIANGLE
Angel	BERMUDA TRIANGLE

Spare Me A Little Of Your Love	BERMUDA TRIANGLE
Sentimental Lady	BERMUDA TRIANGLE
Future Games	BERMUDA TRIANGLE
Why	BERMUDA TRIANGLE
Bermuda Triangle	BERMUDA TRIANGLE
Hypnotized	BERMUDA TRIANGLE

Guitar/Vocals: Bob Welch
Bass: John McVie
Drums: Mick Fleetwood
Keyboards/Vocals: Christine McVie

Producer: —
Engineers: —

BOB WELCH: *I felt like we were just going around in circles. Fleetwood Mac was floundering then, and the essential creative freshness had faded. I thought I needed to strike out on my own and find another context.*

It was during the search for new studios in which to record the follow-up to HEROES ARE HARD TO FIND (which had received a lukewarm reception) that Mick Fleetwood would meet two people who were to have a dramatic effect on the career of Fleetwood Mac.

Lindsey Buckingham and Stevie Nicks had been recording together for a number of years and were currently laying down tracks at Sound City in California when Mick Fleetwood turned up. Keith Olsen played some of their material to demonstrate the facilities available, not aiming to interest Fleetwood in Steve or Lindsey's work, but interested he was.

LINDSEY BUCKINGHAM: *Mick Fleetwood was shopping in a supermarket somewhere and bumped into Thomas Christian. They got to discussing studios – because the group was getting ready to think about another album – and Thomas suggested Sound City in Van Nuys. So Mick went there, and to demonstrate the qualities of the studio, the engineer Keith Olsen played him tracks from our album BUCKINGHAM NICKS which was made there. As it happened Stevie and I were in the next room working on some demos and I went*

in to see Mick stamping his feet to our music. A few weeks later Bob Welch left and we were invited to join.

MICK FLEETWOOD: *I'm a stickler for guitar players. I remember hearing Lindsey's guitar playing and thought it was really good.*
(Behind The Masks)

Initially Mick was only interested in Lindsey Buckingham but on learning that they came as a duo Buckingham and Nicks became full-time members of the tenth line-up of Fleetwood Mac.

MICK FLEETWOOD: *I truly gathered that they came as a package, and they wrote the songs together, you know.*
(Behind The Masks)

LINDSEY BUCKINGHAM: *About a week later, Bob Welch announced that he was leaving – so Mick phoned Keith and asked him if he thought we'd be interested in becoming members of Fleetwood Mac. At the time we were having a New Year's Party at our house. . . wondering if 1975 would be a better year for us – and Keith walked in and said 'Hey, I've got some news. . . Fleetwood Mac want you to join them'. You could have knocked me down with a feather.*
(The Complete Rock Family Trees)

Throughout 1974 Lindsey and Stevie had been working on material for the follow-up to the BUCKINGHAM NICKS album which, unfortunately, had not achieved the success that they or Polydor had hoped for. They took over to Mick Fleetwood demo tapes of material they had been labouring over. These included early versions of 'Landslide', 'Monday Morning', 'I'm So Afraid' and the song that was destined to become a highlight on the forthcoming album and future tours, 'Rhiannon'. Along with a re-recording of 'Crystal', which first appeared on the BUCKINGHAM NICKS album, these tracks were all selected for the new album and the band duly booked into Sound City Studios in February 1975 to start recording. Ten days later the album was in the can.

CHRISTINE MCVIE: *People always remember it ('Rhiannon') – the Welsh Witch thing, the image of Stevie in the hat. Stevie wrote the song before she joined Fleetwood Mac. She writes verses in her journal and she'd written that one and turned it into a demo before she and Lindsey joined the band.*

Sound City Studios.

Guitar: Lindsey Buckingham
Vocals: Stevie Nicks
Bass: John McVie
Drums: Mick Fleetwood
Vocal/Keyboards: Christine McVie

Producer: Fleetwood Mac
Engineer: Keith Olsen

STUDIO SESSIONS FOR WARNER BROTHERS
February–March 1975
Sound City, Van Nuys, California

Rhiannon	A-side/FLEETWOOD MAC
Sugar Daddy	B-side/FLEETWOOD MAC
Monday Morning	B-side/FLEETWOOD MAC
Warm Ways	A-side/FLEETWOOD MAC
Blue Letter	B-side/FLEETWOOD MAC
Over My Head	A-side/FLEETWOOD MAC
Crystal	FLEETWOOD MAC
Say You Love Me	A-side/FLEETWOOD MAC
Landslide	FLEETWOOD MAC
World Turning	FLEETWOOD MAC
I'm So Afraid	B-side/FLEETWOOD MAC

Christine wrote four songs for the album of which three, 'Over My Head', 'Say You Love Me' and the beautiful 'Warm Ways' were all lifted for single release. Two other songs were added during the sessions, 'World Turning', a future showpiece for Mick Fleetwood in their concerts, and the Curtis Brothers' rocker 'Blue Letter', which would subsequently open the album.

Against the wishes of Warner Brothers, who did not want the band to tour before the release of the album, Fleetwood Mac hit the road on 15 May 1975 in El Paso, Texas for the first of a string of concerts that would see the group play throughout Texas, the Mid-West and Northeast. A concert recorded in Passaic, New Jersey found an unofficial release and is an excellent record of how strong the new band were.

RICHARD DASHUT: *After they finished their album, which I'd not worked on much to my dismay, Lindsey called and said 'How would you like to go on the road with Fleetwood Mac?' I looked at my four walls and said, 'yeah, I'll go'. The first gig was in El Paso. I'd never done live sound in my life. I was nervous, very nervous.*

Released while the group were touring, 'Over My Head', in its new remixed version, sold nearly 400,000 copies in its first month of release and squeezed into the American Top Ten in November 1975.

LIVE RECORDINGS
May 1975
Capitol Theatre, Passaic, New Jersey

Station Man	LIVE IN PASSAIC 1975
Spare Me A Little Of Your Love	LIVE IN PASSAIC 1975
Rhiannon	LIVE IN PASSAIC 1975
Landslide	LIVE IN PASSAIC 1975
I'm So Afraid	LIVE IN PASSAIC 1975
World Turning	LIVE IN PASSAIC 1975

The tenth, and most successful, line-up of Fleetwood Mac.

| Don't Let Me Down Again | LIVE IN PASSAIC 1975 |
| Hypnotized | LIVE IN PASSAIC 1975 |

Guitar/Vocals: Lindsey Buckingham
Vocals: Stevie Nicks
Bass: John McVie
Drums: Mick Fleetwood
Keyboards/Vocals: Christine McVie

Producer: —
Engineers: —

As Christmas approached, the band could reflect on a successful year – a Gold Record for FLEETWOOD MAC, a successful tour and four hit singles – and look forward to 1976 with fresh hope, although there were problems ahead.

Unofficial release taken from the 1975 Passaic show radio broadcast.

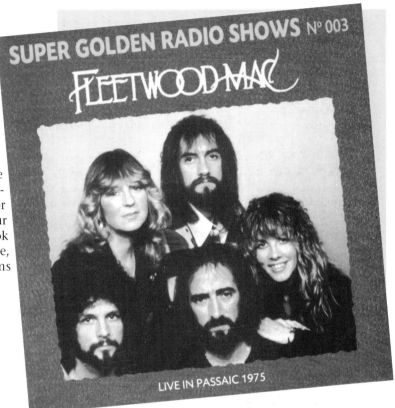

SUPER GOLDEN RADIO SHOWS Nº 003

FLEETWOOD MAC

LIVE IN PASSAIC 1975

RUMOURS – *more than 31 weeks at
number one, worldwide sales in excess
of 35 million, a Grammy Award winner
and a classic album . . . what more
needs to be said?*

YESTERDAY'S GONE
1976–1980

PERSONAL PROBLEMS hit all the members of the band in late 1975, early 1976. Stevie and Lindsey's relationship fell apart, Christine and John's marriage was on the rocks and Mick Fleetwood's marriage was going through a rough time. Even through all the problems, the idea that the band might break up was never mentioned and it was under these conditions that the band began work on the follow-up to FLEETWOOD MAC in the early part of 1976.

JOHN MCVIE: *The energy level within the band slumped each time there was a personnel change – but we got over each successive hump, and our optimism was re-achieved. There was never a sustained period of depression, or else we'd have split up. The highest points were the original bands and the latest line-up.*
(The Complete Rock Family Trees)

LINDSEY BUCKINGHAM: *There was nothing specifically worked out when we went into the studio. We didn't have demo takes. The whole thing just happened.*
(Q Magazine – 1997)

CHRISTINE MCVIE: *When we went in, I thought I was drying up. I was practically panicking because every time I sat down at the piano, nothing came out. Then one day in Sausalito, I just sat down and wrote in the studio, and the four-and-a-half songs of mine on the album are a result of that.*
(Q Magazine – 1997)

STUDIO SESSIONS FOR WARNER BROTHERS
February 1976–December 1976
The Record Plant, Sausalito/Wally Heider Studios, Los Angeles/Davlen Studios, North Hollywood/Criteria Studios, Miami

Second Hand News	RUMOURS
Second Hand News (alternate mix)	25 YEARS – THE CHAIN
Dreams	A-side/RUMOURS
Dreams (alternate mix)	25 YEARS – THE CHAIN
Never Going Back Again	B-side/RUMOURS
Don't Stop	A-side/RUMOURS
Go Your Own Way	A-side/RUMOURS
The Chain	RUMOURS
The Chain (alternate mix)	B-side/ 25 YEARS – THE CHAIN
You Make Loving Fun	A-side/RUMOURS
I Don't Want To Know	RUMOURS
Oh Daddy	RUMOURS
Gold Dust Woman	B-side/RUMOURS
Silver Springs	B-side
Think About It	Unissued
If You Ever Did Believe	Unissued

Guitars/Vocals: Lindsey Buckingham
Vocals: Stevie Nicks
Bass: John McVie
Drums/Percussion: Mick Fleetwood
Vocal/Keyboards/Synthesizer: Christine McVie

The classic RUMOURS *line-up as featured on the back of the sleeve.*

Producer: Fleetwood Mac
Engineer: Richard Dashut/
   Ken Caillat
2nd Engineer: Cris Morris

Session note: As well as the unissued songs 'Think About It' and 'If You Ever Did Believe', Stevie also demoed a number of songs with Lindsey including 'Sorcerer', 'Goldfish And The Ladybug' and 'Sleeping Angel'. These last three tracks have appeared on unofficial tapes. There also exist several vocal out-takes for 'Gold Dust Woman' and 'Silver Springs.'

MICK FLEETWOOD: 'Go Your Own Way's' *rhythm was a tom-tom structure that Lindsey demoed by hitting Kleenex boxes or something. I never quite got to grips with what he wanted, so the end result was my mutated interpretation.*
(Q Magazine – 1997)

RICHARD DASHUT: *The only two instruments that were actually played together on that entire album was the guitar solo and drum track on 'The Chain'.*
(Q Magazine – 1997)

CHRISTINE MCVIE: 'The Chain' *started as the tail end of a jam and we did it all the wrong way round. We kept the end bit and added a new beginning. We used Stevie's lyrics, I created the chorus and Lindsey did the verses. I really don't know how it all came together.*
(Q Magazine – 1997)

CRIS MORRIS: *We were trying to get unique sounds on every instrument. We spent ten hours on a kick drum sound in Studio B. Eventually we moved into Studio A and built a special platform for the drums, which got them sounding the way we wanted.*
(Q Magazine – 1997)

One night after most of the band had left the studio Christine sat down at the piano and played 'Songbird'. Ken Caillat was in the control room and heard the song and felt it needed the depth of a concert hall for the recording. The best live venue in the area was the Berkeley Community Theatre but this was not available and someone suggested using the Zellerback Auditorium instead. With roses spread out on the piano Christine sang the song live on the stage at the Auditorium. It had to be recorded in one take and they spent most of the evening working on the track. The result would become a classic Fleetwood Mac song and one that would feature at the end of their concerts for years to come.

STUDIO SESSION FOR WARNER BROTHERS
3 March 1976
Zellerback Auditorium, U.C. Berkeley

Songbird	B-side/RUMOURS

Vocal/Keyboards: Christine McVie

Producer: Fleetwood Mac
Engineer: Richard Dashut/Ken Caillat
2nd Engineer: Cris Morris

RICHARD DASHUT: *We wore out our original 24-track master. We figured we had 3,000 hours on it and we were losing high end, transients and much of the clarity. The drums were valid and maybe a couple of guitar parts. We ended up transferring all the overdubs on the master to a safety master. We had no sync pulse to lock the two machines together, so we had to manually sync the two machines – ten tracks by ear, using headphones in twelve-hour sessions. People thought we were crazy but it turned out really good.*
(Q Magazine – 1997)

Following the recording of RUMOURS the band hit the road once again. This time, however, they were playing the big outdoor stadiums to thousands of people, young people and young girls who had come to see Stevie Nicks. Many of these concerts were taped for possible future release.

SOUNDCHECK RECORDINGS FOR WARNER BROTHERS
1977
Palais De Sport, Paris

Dreams	A-side/FLEETWOOD MAC LIVE
Don't Stop	FLEETWOOD MAC LIVE

Guitar/Vocals: Lindsey Buckingham
Vocals: Stevie Nicks
Bass: John McVie
Drums: Mick Fleetwood
Keyboards/Vocals: Christine McVie

Producer: Fleetwood Mac
Engineers: Ken Caillat/Biff Dawes/Richard Dashut/Trip Khalaf

LIVE RECORDINGS FOR WARNER BROTHERS
1977
Tokyo

Monday Morning	B-side/
	FLEETWOOD MAC LIVE
Oh Well	*Unissued*
Rhiannon	*Unissued*
Over My Head	*Unissued*
Go Your Own Way	*Unissued*
World Turning	*Unissued*
The Chain	*Unissued*
Songbird	*Unissued*

Guitar/Vocals: Lindsey Buckingham
Vocals: Stevie Nicks
Bass: John McVie
Drums: Mick Fleetwood
Keyboards/Vocals: Christine McVie

Producer: Fleetwood Mac
Engineers: Ken Caillat/Richard Dashut

At the Grammy Awards Ceremony, held in February, Fleetwood Mac took Album Of The Year for RUMOURS, and were runner-up in the Best Arrangement For Voices category with 'Go Your Own Way'. The Eagles took the honours with 'New Kid In Town'. These weren't the only awards though. In the prestigious Rolling Stone Awards, Fleetwood Mac received four awards – Artists Of The Year, Band Of The Year, Best Album (RUMOURS) and Best Single ('Dreams'), as well as making it onto the cover of the magazine.

LIVE RECORDINGS FOR WARNER BROTHERS
1977
Passaic

Don't Let Me Down   FLEETWOOD MAC LIVE

Guitar/Vocals: Lindsey Buckingham
Vocals: Stevie Nicks
Bass: John McVie
Drums: Mick Fleetwood
Keyboards/Vocals: Christine McVie

Producer: Fleetwood Mac
Engineers: Ken Caillat/Richard Dashut

During his time in the UK, Lindsey had been listening to many of the new bands, including the Clash, and was determined that their next album would be nothing like RUMOURS. The previous sessions had been hard, especially the travelling around various studios to create the right sound and so suggestions were made that they build their own studio, an idea that was dropped in favour of building a new studio at Village Recorders.

STUDIO SESSIONS FOR WARNER BROTHERS
May–July 1978/Late 1978–Early Summer 1979
Studio D, Village Recorders, Los Angeles

Brown Eyes   TUSK
Over & Over   TUSK
The Ledge   TUSK
Think About Me   A-side/TUSK
Save Me A Place   B-side/TUSK
Sara   A-side/TUSK

Another award ceremony!

What Makes You Think You're The One	TUSK
Storms	TUSK
That's All For Everyone	TUSK
Not That Funny	A-side/TUSK
Sisters Of The Moon	A-side (US)/TUSK
Angel	TUSK
Angel *(alternate mix)*	25 YEARS – THE CHAIN
That's Enough For Me	B-side/TUSK
Never Make Me Cry	B-side/TUSK
I Know I'm Not Wrong	TUSK
Honey Hi	B-side (US)/TUSK
Beautiful Child	TUSK
Beautiful Child *(alternate mix)*	25 YEARS – THE CHAIN
Walk A Thin Line	B-side (US)/TUSK
Tusk	A-side/TUSK
Tusk *(USC Intro Mix)*	25 YEARS – THE CHAIN
Never Forget	TUSK
The Dealer	*Unissued*
Out On The Road	*Unissued*
Watchdevil	*Unissued*
24 Karat	*Unissued*
Cecilia	*Unissued*
Lady From The Mountain	*Unissued*

Guitar: Peter Green ('Brown Eyes' only)
Guitar: Lindsey Buckingham
Vocals: Stevie Nicks
Piano: Stevie Nicks ('Sara' only)
Bass: John McVie
Drums: Mick Fleetwood
Vocal/Keyboards: Christine McVie

Producer: Fleetwood Mac
Engineer: Richard Dashut/ Ken Caillat

Session note: As well as the unissued songs from these sessions Stevie demoed several other songs for possible inclusion.

'Tusk' began life as a riff the band used to play on stage and attempts were made to record the track early on but it would be several months later that the group would return to the song. The idea to use a marching band had been Mick's. While in France he had been awoken by the sound of the local band playing in the courtyard and his idea was to use the local marching band in each city they played during the forthcoming tour. They would appear with the group on stage during the song 'Tusk'. Logistics prevented this but they did use the USC Trojan Marching Band on the single. Their part was recorded, and filmed, at Dodger Stadium.

Mick Fleetwood: *This ('Tusk') started off being a jam, the sort of thing we done at warm-ups. Originally it was a lot slower than the recorded version – about half that tempo. . . it seemed logical to turn it into something.*
(Record Hunter, February 1992)

CD sleeve for the double album TUSK, *the follow-up to* RUMOURS.

SESSION FOR WARNER BROTHERS
1978
Dodger Stadium, California

Tusk   A-side/Tusk

The USC Trojan Marching Band

Producer: Fleetwood Mac
Engineer: Richard Dashut/Ken Caillat

Recording sessions for the new album finished
in the summer and they were faced with the
fact that they had too many good songs to
release on just a single album and approached
Warner's regarding releasing all the tracks as a
double set. Warner's were concerned about
sales if they went along with the band's plan
but eventually gave in. Whilst not achieving
the sales of RUMOURS the album went on to sell
over 4 million copies.

right *Stevie and Lindsey at the Hollywood
Star presentation.*

below *Fleetwood Mac accepting their Hollywood
Star.*

Following the recording of TUSK Fleetwood Mac hit the road for what was to be their longest and most arduous tour to date. The set list on this tour included 'Say You Love Me', 'The Chain', 'Don't Stop', 'Oh Well', 'Dreams', 'Sara', 'Rhiannon', 'Landslide', 'Not That Funny', 'That's Enough For Me', 'Oh Daddy, I'm So Afraid', 'Never Going Back Again', 'Tusk', 'You Make Loving Fun', 'Angel', 'World Turning', 'Go Your Own Way', 'Sisters Of The Moon' and 'Songbird'. Many of the shows were recorded for future release and the following entries only detail the tracks that made it to the final album selection. It is unclear what and how much unreleased material remains in the vaults.

RICHARD DASHUT: *We will not do a live album because we believe that live music and studio sound are two different things. I personally do not like live albums. I would rather go to a concert and feel it rather than hear a recording of it.*
(Behind The Masks)

CLIFFORD DAVIS: *My feeling about good live albums is this. Sometimes you can get an artist who, no matter how they sounded in the studio, simply excel live. And Fleetwood Mac made their name as a live band.*
(Behind The Masks)

TOUR REHEARSALS FOR THE TUSK TOUR
Autumn 1979
Sunset Gower Studio Complex

The Chain	Unissued
Oh Well	Unissued
Dreams	Unissued
Not That Funny	Unissued
Rhiannon	Unissued
Over And Over	Unissued
The Ledge	Unissued
Sara	Unissued
What Makes You Think You're The One	Unissued

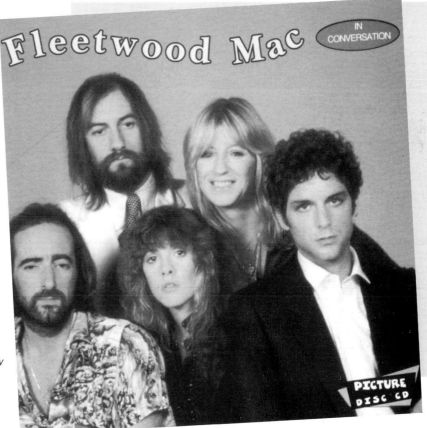

CD cover for unofficial interview disc. This release featured a picture disc.

Save Me A Place	*Unissued*
Landslide	*Unissued*
Oh Daddy	*Unissued*
Angel	*Unissued*
You Make Loving Fun	*Unissued*
I'm So Afraid	*Unissued*
World Turning	*Unissued*
Go Your Own Way	*Unissued*
Tusk	*Unissued*
Sisters Of The Moon	*Unissued*
I Know I'm Not Wrong	*Unissued*
Songbird	*Unissued*

Guitar/Vocals: Lindsey Buckingham
Vocals: Stevie Nicks
Bass: John McVie
Drums: Mick Fleetwood
Keyboards/Vocals: Christine McVie

These recordings of rehearsals for the forth-coming Tusk tour appeared on an unofficial video tape.

Just before the start of the tour Fleetwood Mac were honoured with the 157th Star on Hollywood's Walk Of Fame and the day was proclaimed Fleetwood Mac Day.

LIVE RECORDINGS FOR WARNER BROTHERS
5–6 November 1979
Checker Dome, St. Louis

Oh Well	FLEETWOOD MAC LIVE
Sara	FLEETWOOD MAC LIVE

Guitar/Vocals: Lindsey Buckingham
Vocals: Stevie Nicks
Bass: John McVie
Drums: Mick Fleetwood
Keyboards/Vocals: Christine McVie
Guitar: Ray Lindsey
Percussion: Tony Todaro
Keyboards: Jeffrey Sova

Producer: Fleetwood Mac
Engineers: Ken Caillat/Biff Dawes/Richard
   Dashut/Trip Khalaf

LIVE RECORDINGS FOR WARNER BROTHERS
June 1980
Wembley Arena, London

Rhiannon	FLEETWOOD MAC LIVE
Landslide	FLEETWOOD MAC LIVE

Guitar/Vocals: Lindsey Buckingham
Vocals: Stevie Nicks
Bass: John McVie
Drums: Mick Fleetwood
Keyboards/Vocals: Christine McVie
Guitar: Ray Lindsey
Percussion: Tony Todaro
Keyboards: Jeffrey Sova

Producer: Fleetwood Mac
Engineers: Ken Caillat/Biff Dawes/Richard
   Dashut/Trip Khalaf

MICK FLEETWOOD: *It's a prime example of a song that developed over the years – well, almost immediately really. There's a version on the live album that's so different. 'Rhiannon' really became something of a party piece for Stevie. It became amped-up, vocally and instrumentally, until it became a real ball-buster. A highlight of the shows of that period.*

STUDIO SESSIONS FOR WARNER BROTHERS (Overdubs only)
July 1980
George Massenburg Studios

Monday Morning	FLEETWOOD MAC LIVE
Say You Love Me	FLEETWOOD MAC LIVE
Dreams	FLEETWOOD MAC LIVE
Oh Well	FLEETWOOD MAC LIVE
Rhiannon	FLEETWOOD MAC LIVE
Don't Stop	FLEETWOOD MAC LIVE
Don't Let Me Down Again	FLEETWOOD MAC LIVE
Sara	FLEETWOOD MAC LIVE

Guitar/Vocals: Lindsey Buckingham
Vocals: Stevie Nicks

BARRY DICKINS & ROD MACSWEEN FOR ITB PRESENT

FLEETWOOD MAC

IN CONCERT

CHRISTINE McVIE · STEVIE NICKS · MICK FLEETWOOD · LINDSEY BUCKINGHAM · JOHN McVIE

20th ~~SOLD OUT~~ 22nd JUNE
25th & 26th JUNE at 7.30pm

WEMBLEY ARENA

Tickets: £7.50 £6.50 £5.50

available from MAC Promotions, P.O Box 2BZ, London W1A 2BZ.
(send cheques or postal orders payable to MAC Promotions with stamped addressed
envelope. Please state date preference and allow 21 days for delivery.)

Tour ad for their successful five-nights at Wembley Arena in 1980.

Bass: John McVie
Drums: Mick Fleetwood
Keyboards/Vocals: Christine McVie
Guitar: Ray Lindsey
Percussion: Tony Todaro
Keyboards: Jeffrey Sova

Producer: Fleetwood Mac
Engineers: Ken Caillat/Biff Dawes/Richard
    Dashut/Trip Khalaf

**LIVE RECORDINGS FOR WARNER
BROTHERS
1980
Santa Monica**

One More Night   FLEETWOOD MAC LIVE
Fireflies   A-side (US)/
                                       FLEETWOOD MAC LIVE
Farmers Daughter   A-side (US)/
                                       FLEETWOOD MAC LIVE

Guitar/Vocals: Lindsey Buckingham
Vocals: Stevie Nicks
Bass: John McVie
Drums: Mick Fleetwood
Keyboards/Vocals: Christine McVie
Guitar: Ray Lindsey
Percussion: Tony Todaro
Keyboards: Jeffrey Sova

Producer: Fleetwood Mac
Engineers: Ken Caillat/Biff Dawes/Richard
   Dashut/Trip Khalaf

LIVE RECORDINGS FOR WARNER BROTHERS
22 August 1980
Myriad, Oklahoma City

Over And Over   FLEETWOOD MAC LIVE

Guitar/Vocals: Lindsey
   Buckingham
Vocals: Stevie Nicks
Bass: John McVie
Drums: Mick Fleetwood
Keyboards/Vocals: Christine
   McVie
Guitar: Ray Lindsey
Percussion: Tony Todaro
Keyboards: Jeffrey Sova

Producer: Fleetwood Mac
Engineers: Ken Caillat/Biff
   Dawes/Richard Dashut/
   Trip Khalaf

*Material from their
year-long tour was
released on this double-
album. (The CD re-issue
is shown here)*

LIVE RECORDINGS FOR WARNER BROTHERS
23 August 1980
Kansas Coliseum, Witchita

Say You Love Me   FLEETWOOD MAC LIVE

Guitar/Vocals: Lindsey Buckingham
Vocals: Stevie Nicks
Bass: John McVie
Drums: Mick Fleetwood
Keyboards/Vocals: Christine McVie
Guitar: Ray Lindsey
Percussion: Tony Todaro
Keyboards: Jeffrey Sova

Producer: Fleetwood Mac
Engineers: Ken Caillat/Biff Dawes/Richard
   Dashut/Trip Khalaf

LIVE RECORDINGS FOR WARNER BROTHERS
24 August 1980
Kemper Arena, Kansas City

Over My Head   FLEETWOOD MAC LIVE

Guitar/Vocals: Lindsey Buckingham
Vocals: Stevie Nicks
Bass: John McVie
Drums: Mick Fleetwood
Keyboards/Vocals: Christine McVie
Guitar: Ray Lindsey
Percussion: Tony Todaro
Keyboards: Jeffrey Sova

Producer: Fleetwood Mac
Engineers: Ken Caillat/Biff Dawes/Richard
   Dashut/Trip Khalaf

LIVE RECORDINGS FOR WARNER BROTHERS
28 August 1980
McKale Center, Tucson

Never Going Back Again   FLEETWOOD MAC LIVE

Guitar/Vocals: Lindsey Buckingham
Vocals: Stevie Nicks
Bass: John McVie
Drums: Mick Fleetwood
Keyboards/Vocals: Christine McVie
Guitar: Ray Lindsey
Percussion: Tony Todaro
Keyboards: Jeffrey Sova

Producer: Fleetwood Mac
Engineers: Ken Caillat/Biff Dawes/Richard
   Dashut/Trip Khalaf

LIVE RECORDINGS FOR WARNER BROTHERS
1980
Cleveland

Not That Funny   FLEETWOOD MAC LIVE
I'm So Afraid   FLEETWOOD MAC LIVE
Go Your Own Way   FLEETWOOD MAC LIVE

Guitar/Vocals: Lindsey Buckingham
Vocals: Stevie Nicks
Bass: John McVie
Drums: Mick Fleetwood
Keyboards/Vocals: Christine McVie
Guitar: Ray Lindsey
Percussion: Tony Todaro
Keyboards: Jeffrey Sova

Producer: Fleetwood Mac
Engineers: Ken Caillat/Biff Dawes/Richard
   Dashut/Trip Khalaf

MICK FLEETWOOD: *Fleetwood Mac has never done a live album before with any form of this band. It seemed to me that after a year on the road, there was no better time to release one.*
(Behind The Masks)

Many more shows were recorded and remain in the vaults. For the sake of clarity only the material released is listed here.

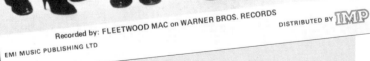

Sheet music cover for 'Big Love'.

NOT JUST A MIRAGE
1981–1990

IN 1981, following a brief lay-off during which time Stevie Nicks recorded the hugely successful album BELLA DONNA and both Mick and Lindsey had worked on solo projects the band regrouped and found themselves working in France on the basic tracks for what was to become the follow-up to TUSK.

CHRISTINE McVIE: *We decided we wanted to be outside of Los Angeles because we wanted to be without any distractions. We wanted to be just the five of us, and work something out.*
(Behind The Masks)

STUDIO SESSIONS FOR WARNER BROTHERS
May–June 1981
Le Chateau, Herouville, France

Love In Store	*Basic Tracks Only – See June–December 1981*
Can't Go Back	*Basic Tracks Only – See June–December 1981*
That's Alright	*Basic Tracks Only – See June–December 1981*
Book Of Love	*Basic Tracks Only – See June–December 1981*
Gypsy	*Basic Tracks Only – See June–December 1981*
Only Over You	*Basic Tracks Only – See June–December 1981*
Empire State	*Basic Tracks Only – See June–December 1981*
Straight Back	*Basic Tracks Only – See June–December 1981*
Hold Me	*Basic Tracks Only – See June–December 1981*
Oh Diane	*Basic Tracks Only – See June–December 1981*
Eyes Of The World	*Basic Tracks Only – See June–December 1981*
Wish You Were Here	*Basic Tracks Only – See June–December 1981*
Cool, Clear Water	*Basic Tracks Only – See June–December 1981*
Make Me A Mask	*Basic Tracks Only – See June–December 1981*
Teen Beat	*Basic Tracks Only – See June–December 1981*
Goodbye Angel	*Basic Tracks Only – See June–December 1981*
Smile At You (version # 1)	*Unissued*
Smile At You (version # 2)	*Unissued*
If You Were My Love	*Unissued*

Guitar/Vocals: Lindsey Buckingham
Vocals: Stevie Nicks
Bass: John McVie
Drums: Mick Fleetwood
Keyboards/Vocals: Christine McVie

Producer: Lindsey Buckingham/
Engineers: Lindsey Buckingham/Richard Dashut/ Ken Caillat

Lindsey had been working on his solo album, LAW AND ORDER, and brought 'Can't Let Go' and 'Eyes Of The World' to the sessions while Stevie contributed a song she'd saved from her BELLA DONNA album, 'Gypsy'. Three tracks – 'Book Of Love', 'Empire State' and 'Oh Diane' were written in the studio during the sessions.

OVERDUB SESSIONS FOR WARNER BROTHERS
June–December 1981
Larrabee Sound, Los Angeles/The Record Plant, Los Angeles

Love In Store	A-side (US)/MIRAGE
Can't Go Back	A-side/MIRAGE
That's Alright	B-side/MIRAGE
Book Of Love	MIRAGE
Gypsy	A-side/MIRAGE
Only Over You	B-side/MIRAGE
Empire State	MIRAGE
Straight Back	MIRAGE
Hold Me	A-side/MIRAGE
Oh Diane	A-side/MIRAGE
Eyes Of The World	B-side/MIRAGE
Wish You Were Here	MIRAGE
Cool, Clear Water	B-side
Make Me A Mask	THE CHAIN-SELECTIONS FROM 25 YEARS
Teen Beat	THE CHAIN-SELECTIONS FROM 25 YEARS
Goodbye Angel	THE CHAIN-SELECTIONS FROM 25 YEARS

Guitar/Vocals: Lindsey Buckingham
Vocals: Stevie Nicks
Bass: John McVie
Drums: Mick Fleetwood
Keyboards/Vocals: Christine McVie

Producer: Lindsey Buckingham/
Engineers: Lindsey Buckingham/Richard Dashut/
  Ken Caillat

The first single lifted from the album, 'Hold Me' was a US hit, helped along by a video which was broadcast on MTV. In the UK 'Oh Diane' was a top ten success for the group.

LINDSEY BUCKINGHAM: *We should have progressed but instead we just reacted against* TUSK. *It was pleasant but much too safe.* MIRAGE *was quite reactionary after* Tusk, *I think, because forces within the band and without were saying to me 'You went too far on* TUSK'. *That was kind of hard to deal with, taking the flak over* TUSK.
(Behind The Masks)

Following the recording of the album Fleetwood Mac hit the road once again. Rehearsals were held in July 1982 and on 1 September the tour opened in Greensboro', North Carolina and closed in Oakland, California on the 30th, a short tour when compared with the mammoth Tusk Tour two years earlier. The set list on this tour included 'Second Hand News', 'The Chain', 'Don't Stop', 'Dreams', 'Oh Well!', 'Rhiannon', 'Brown Eyes', 'Eyes Of The World', 'Gypsy', 'Love In Store', 'Not That Funny', 'Landslide', 'Tusk', 'Sara', 'Hold Me', 'You Make Lovin' Fun', 'I'm So Afraid', 'Go Your Own Way', 'Blue Letter', 'Sisters Of The Moon' and 'Songbird'. Two shows on 21 and 22 October were filmed for future video release.

LIVE RECORDINGS FOR VIDEO RELEASE
21–22 OCTOBER 1982
Forum, Los Angeles

The Chain	FLEETWOOD MAC IN CONCERT VIDEO
Gypsy	FLEETWOOD MAC IN CONCERT VIDEO
Love In Store	FLEETWOOD MAC IN CONCERT VIDEO
Not That Funny	FLEETWOOD MAC IN CONCERT VIDEO
You Make Loving Fun	FLEETWOOD MAC IN CONCERT VIDEO
I'm So Afraid	FLEETWOOD MAC IN CONCERT VIDEO
Blue Letter	FLEETWOOD MAC IN CONCERT VIDEO
Rhiannon	FLEETWOOD MAC IN CONCERT VIDEO
Tusk	FLEETWOOD MAC IN CONCERT VIDEO

The video cover of
The Mirage Tour.

Eyes Of The World	FLEETWOOD MAC IN CONCERT VIDEO
Go Your Own Way	FLEETWOOD MAC IN CONCERT VIDEO
Sisters Of The Moon	FLEETWOOD MAC IN CONCERT VIDEO
Songbird	FLEETWOOD MAC IN CONCERT VIDEO

Guitar/Vocals: Lindsey Buckingham
Vocals: Stevie Nicks
Bass: John McVie
Drums: Mick Fleetwood
Keyboards/Vocals: Christine McVie

Producer: Mickey Shapiro/Mick Fleetwood
Engineers: Ken Caillat

A three year lay-off saw various members of the group working on solo projects. Stevie released two very successful albums – WILD HEART and ROCK A LITTLE while Lindsey finished work on LAW AND ORDER and also released GO INSANE. Mick Fleetwood, influenced by South African rhythms, released two solo efforts THE VISITOR and I'M NOT ME, the latter under the group name Mick Fleetwood's Zoo.

It was ironic that a solo outing would see Fleetwood Mac together again and go on to record one of their most successful albums. Christine had been approached to record the Elvis classic 'Can't Help Falling In Love' for the soundtrack of the film *A Fine Mess*. She called Richard Dashut in to produce the track who, knowing that Lindsey was a big Elvis fan, asked him to play on the track. With the addition of Mick and John four-fifths of the band were together again in the studio.

STUDIO SESSIONS FOR WARNER BROTHERS
August 1985
Studio Unknown

Can't Help Falling In Love	A FINE MESS (soundtrack)

Keyboards/Vocals: Christine McVie
Guitars/Vocals: Lindsey Buckingham
Bass: John McVie
Drums: Mick Fleetwood

Producer: Richard Dashut
Engineers: —

Returning to the familiar formula, Fleetwood Mac started work on what was to become their most successful album since RUMOURS, nearly ten years earlier.

STUDIO SESSIONS FOR WARNER BROTHERS
Late 1985–Early 1986
Rumbo Recorders, Canoga Park, California

Big Love	*Basic Tracks Only – See 1986–January 1987*
Seven Wonders	*Basic Tracks Only – See 1986–January 1987*
Everywhere	*Basic Tracks Only – See 1986–January 1987*
Caroline	*Basic Tracks Only – See 1986–January 1987*
Tango In The Night	*Basic Tracks Only – See 1986–January 1987*
Mystified	*Basic Tracks Only – See 1986–January 1987*
Little Lies	*Basic Tracks Only – See 1986–January 1987*
Family Man	*Basic Tracks Only – See 1986–January 1987*
Welcome To The Room. . . Sara	*Basic Tracks Only – See 1986–January 1987*
Isn't It Midnight	*Basic Tracks Only – See 1986–January 1987*
When I See You Again	*Basic Tracks Only – See 1986–January 1987*
You And I, Part I	*Basic Tracks Only – See 1986–January 1987*
You And I, Part II	*Basic Tracks Only – See 1986–January 1987*

Another press launch, this time for Christine McVie's solo album.

Book Of Miracles	*Basic Tracks Only – See 1986–January 1987*
Ricky	*Basic Tracks Only – See 1986–January 1987*
Down Endless Street	*Basic Tracks Only – See 1986–January 1987*
Family Party (Bonus Beats)	*Basic Tracks Only – See 1986–January 1987*
Juliet	*Unissued*

Guitars/Vocals: Lindsey Buckingham
Vocals: Stevie Nicks
Bass: John McVie
Drums: Mick Fleetwood
Keyboards/Vocals: Christine McVie

Producer: Lindsey Buckingham/Richard Dashut
Engineers: Greg Droman/Lindsey Buckingham

Nile Rogers and Jason Casaro had been approached to produce the new album but were not successful so the band went back to the old tradition of producing the album themselves.

OVERDUB SESSIONS FOR WARNER BROTHERS
1986–January 1987
The Slope

Big Love	A-side/ TANGO IN THE NIGHT
Seven Wonders	A-side/ TANGO IN THE NIGHT
Everywhere	A-side/ TANGO IN THE NIGHT
Caroline	TANGO IN THE NIGHT
Tango In The Night	TANGO IN THE NIGHT
Mystified	B-side/ TANGO IN THE NIGHT
Little Lies	A-side/ TANGO IN THE NIGHT
Family Man	A-side/ TANGO IN THE NIGHT
Welcome To The Room . . . Sara	TANGO IN THE NIGHT

'Songbird' – Christine McVie.

Isn't It Midnight	A-side/
	TANGO IN THE NIGHT
Isn't It Midnight	25 YEARS – THE CHAIN
(edited alternate version)	
When I See You Again	B-side/
	TANGO IN THE NIGHT
You And I, Part I	B-side
You And I, Part II	B-side/
	TANGO IN THE NIGHT
Book Of Miracles	B-side
Ricky	B-side
Down Endless Street	B-side
Family Party (Bonus Beats)	B-side
Juliet	Unissued
What Has Rock And Roll	
. . . Ever Done For You?	Unissued

Guitars/Vocals: Lindsey Buckingham
Vocals: Stevie Nicks
Bass: John McVie
Drums: Mick Fleetwood
Keyboards/Vocals: Christine McVie

Producer: Lindsey Buckingham/Richard Dashut
Engineers: Greg Droman/Lindsey Buckingham

The Slope was Lindsey's own studio built in the garage of his home.

Session note: Lindsey Buckingham's arrangement of 'Juliet' was released as 'Book Of Miracles.'

Again Lindsey brought in some of his songs that were intended for a solo project – 'Big Love' (which would become the first single lifted from the album) 'Caroline', 'Tango In The Night' and 'Family Man'. Christine wrote three tracks that would all become hit singles when released – 'Everywhere', 'Little Lies' and 'Isn't It Midnight'. Stevie contributed 'Welcome To The Room. . . Sara' and 'Seven Wonders'.

TANGO IN THE NIGHT received favourable reviews – 'Fleetwood Mac shimmers back' (Rolling Stone) and 'A mood of edgy, sophisticated wistfulness' and 'exquisitely produced' (New York Times).

Fleetwood Mac were definitely back.

Following the recording it was time to hit the road once again, only this time Lindsey Buckingham would not be going along. Unhappy with touring and wanting to develop his solo projects Buckingham felt it was time to leave. The recording of TANGO IN THE NIGHT had already interrupted his solo work and to commit himself to months out on the road was just not feasible.

Finding a replacement was not a major problem. Both Rick Vito and Billy Burnette had worked with various members of the group on and off over the past few years.

In September Fleetwood Mac rehearsed with new members Rick Vito and Billy Burnette at a studio in California. Their first session as the 'new boys' in the group followed with both tracks appearing on the bands GREATEST HITS package.

Stevie Nicks

STUDIO SESSION FOR WARNER BROTHERS
Late 1987
Studio Unknown

No Questions Asked	B-side/Greatest Hits
As Long As You Follow	A-side/Greatest Hits

Guitar/Vocals: Rick Vito
Guitar/Vocals: Billy Burnette
Vocals: Stevie Nicks
Bass: John McVie
Drums/Percussion: Mick Fleetwood
Keyboards/Vocals: Christine McVie

Producer: Greg Ladanyi/Fleetwood Mac
Engineers: Greg Ladanyi

Session note: 'No Questions Asked' was a solo track intended for Stevie Nicks' fourth album The Other Side Of The Mirror, but she gave it over to Fleetwood Mac for inclusion on the Greatest Hits album. The album version fades out but in the studio the song lasted longer with extra lyrics.

The set list for the Shake The Cage Tour included the following titles: 'Say You Love Me', 'The Chain', 'Dreams', 'Isn't It Midnight', 'Oh Well', 'Rhiannon', 'Seven Wonders', 'Rattlesnake Shake', 'Gypsy', 'Over My Head', 'Gold Dust Woman', 'Has Anyone Ever Written Anything For You', 'I Loved Another Woman', 'Brown Eyes', 'Don't Let Me Down Again', 'World Turning', 'Little Lies', 'Stand Back', 'You Make Loving Fun', 'Don't Stop', 'Blue Letter', 'Go Your Own Way' and 'Songbird'.

LIVE RECORDINGS FOR VIDEO RELEASE
12–13 December 1987
Cow Palace, San Fransisco

The Chain	Tango In The Night Video
Everywhere	Tango In The Night Video
Dreams	Tango In The Night Video
Seven Wonders	Tango In The Night Video
Isn't It Midnight	Tango In The Night Video

New members Rick Vito and Billy Burnette.

The 1987 tour programme.

Stevie Nicks

World Turning	TANGO IN THE NIGHT VIDEO
Little Lies	TANGO IN THE NIGHT VIDEO
Oh Well	TANGO IN THE NIGHT VIDEO
Gold Dust Woman	TANGO IN THE NIGHT VIDEO
Another Woman	TANGO IN THE NIGHT VIDEO
Standback	TANGO IN THE NIGHT VIDEO
Songbird	TANGO IN THE NIGHT VIDEO
Don't Stop	TANGO IN THE NIGHT VIDEO

Guitar/Vocals: Billy Burnette
Guitar/Vocals: Rick Vito
Vocals: Stevie Nicks
Bass: John McVie
Drums: Mick Fleetwood
Keyboards/Vocals: Christine McVie
Percussion: Asante
Back-up Singers: Sharon Celani/Lori Perry/
   Eliscia Wright

Producer: John B House
Engineers: Bruce Jackson

LIVE RECORDINGS FOR WARNER BROTHERS
Possibly 12–13 December 1987
Cow Palace, San Fransisco

Oh Well	B-side
Another Woman	B-side
Everywhere	B-side
Little Lies	B-side
The Chain	B-side

Guitar/Vocals: Billy Burnette
Guitar/Vocals: Rick Vito
Vocals: Stevie Nicks
Bass: John McVie
Drums: Mick Fleetwood
Keyboards/Vocals: Christine McVie
Percussion: Asante
Back-up Singers: Sharon Celani/Lori Perry/
   Eliscia Wright

Producer: Fleetwood Mac/Dennis Mays
Engineers:

It is more than likely that the above titles come from the same show that was filmed for video release.

Following the tour it was time to record a new album, the first with Vito and Burnette, although they had recorded two tracks for inclusion on the GREATEST HITS package.

STUDIO SESSIONS FOR WARNER BROTHERS
The Complex, Los Angeles & Vintage Recorders, Phoenix
15 January 1989–Late 1989

Skies The Limit	A-side/
	BEHIND THE MASK
Love Is Dangerous	BEHIND THE MASK
In The Back Of My Mind	A-side/
	BEHIND THE MASK
Do You Know	BEHIND THE MASK
Save Me	A-side/
	BEHIND THE MASK
Affairs Of The Heart	BEHIND THE MASK

When The Sun Goes Down	BEHIND THE MASK
Behind The Mask	BEHIND THE MASK
Stand On The Rock	BEHIND THE MASK
Hard Feelings	A-side (US)/ BEHIND THE MASK
Freedom	B-side (US)/ BEHIND THE MASK
When It Comes To Love	BEHIND THE MASK
The Second Time	B-side/ BEHIND THE MASK
Freedom	B-side
Lizard People	B-side

Guitar/Vocals: Rick Vito
Guitar/Vocals: Billy Burnette
Vocals: Stevie Nicks
Bass: John McVie
Drums/Percussion: Mick Fleetwood
Keyboards/Vocals: Christine McVie

Producer: Greg Ladanyi/Fleetwood Mac
Engineers: Greg Ladanyi

With the new album recorded it was time once again for The Mac to hit the road. The Behind The Mask Tour had kicked off with concerts in Australia in March, with the US leg of the tour taking up most of June. By September, following a string of dates in Europe, they were back in the UK making appearances at Wembley Arena, London and Maine Road, Manchester. This concert was recorded and broadcast live by Radio 1 and would find an unofficicial release as NEXT STOP: MAINE ROAD.

SESSION FOR RADIO 1
25 August 1990
Maine Road, Manchester

In The Back Of My Mind	Radio Broadcast
The Chain	Radio Broadcast/ NEXT STOP: MAINE ROAD

Fleetwood Mac at the MTV Video Music awards.

Dreams	Radio Broadcast/ NEXT STOP: MAINE ROAD
Isn't It Midnight	Radio Broadcast/ NEXT STOP: MAINE ROAD
Oh Well	Radio Broadcast/ NEXT STOP: MAINE ROAD
Rhiannon	Radio Broadcast/ NEXT STOP: MAINE ROAD
Stop Messin' Round	NEXT STOP: MAINE ROAD
Save Me	Radio Broadcast/ NEXT STOP: MAINE ROAD
Gold Dust Woman	Radio Broadcast/ NEXT STOP: MAINE ROAD
Another Woman	Radio Broadcast/ NEXT STOP: MAINE ROAD
Landslide	Radio Broadcast/ NEXT STOP: MAINE ROAD
World Turning	NEXT STOP: MAINE ROAD
Everywhere	Radio Broadcast/ NEXT STOP: MAINE ROAD
Stand On The Rock	Radio Broadcast/ NEXT STOP: MAINE ROAD
Little Lies	Radio Broadcast/ NEXT STOP: MAINE ROAD
Stand Back	Radio Broadcast/ NEXT STOP: MAINE ROAD
You Make Loving Fun	Radio Broadcast/ NEXT STOP: MAINE ROAD

Go Your Own Way	NEXT STOP: MAINE ROAD
Tear It Up	NEXT STOP: MAINE ROAD
Don't Stop	NEXT STOP: MAINE ROAD

Guitar/Vocals: Rick Vito
Guitar/Vocals: Billy Burnette
Vocals: Stevie Nicks
Bass: John McVie
Drums/Percussion: Mick Fleetwood
Keyboards/Vocals: Christine McVie

Producer: —
Engineers: —

left *Programme for the Behind The Mask world tour, 1990.*

right *Advertisement for the Behind The Mask tour.*

Mick Fleetwood in New York, 1992.

NEVER BREAK THE CHAIN
1991–1997

DURING 1990-1991 Christine McVie, Stevie Nicks and Rick Vito would all leave Fleetwood Mac, although they all worked together on tracks for the 25th anniversary set THE CHAIN.

Billy Burnette

STUDIO SESSIONS FOR WARNER BROTHERS
1991
Studio Unknown

Paper Doll   THE CHAIN-SELECTIONS
                          FROM 25 YEARS

Guitar/Vocals: Rick Vito
Guitar/Vocals: Billy Burnette
Vocals: Stevie Nicks
Bass: John McVie
Drums/Percussion: Mick Fleetwood
Keyboards/Vocals: Christine McVie

Producer: Richard Dashut
Engineers: Robert Hart/Richard Ornstein

STUDIO SESSIONS FOR WARNER BROTHERS
1991
Studio Unknown

Love Shines   A-side/
                          THE CHAIN-SELECTIONS
                            FROM 25 YEARS
Heart Of Stone   THE CHAIN-SELECTIONS
                            FROM 25 YEARS

Guitar/Vocals: Rick Vito
Guitar/Vocals: Billy Burnette
Vocals: Stevie Nicks
Bass: John McVie

Drums/Percussion: Mick Fleetwood
Keyboards/Vocals: Christine McVie

Producer: Patrick Leonard
Engineers: Robert Hart/Richard Ornstein

LIVE BROADCAST
19 January 1993
Capital Center, Landover, MD

Don't Stop   TV Broadcast

Guitar/Vocals: Lindsey Buckingham
Vocals: Stevie Nicks
Bass: John McVie
Drums: Mick Fleetwood
Keyboards/Vocals: Christine McVie

Producer: —
Engineers: —

The original RUMOURS line-up reformed for President Clinton's Inaugural Gala, at his special request, and performed his favourite song. It was the first time this line-up had appeared on stage for nearly a decade.

With a new line-up that included ex-Traffic vocalist Dave Mason and Bekka Bramlett, daughter of Delaney and Bonnie Bramlett, Fleetwood Mac recorded TIME, their least successful album. A tour as part of a nostalgia package with Pat Benatar and REO Speedwagon did little to help and soon after the band would split.

left *Stevie Nicks*
above *Mick Fleetwood at the Brit Awards in 1992.*

STUDIO SESSIONS FOR WARNER BROTHERS
1995
Ocean Way Recording, Hollywood and Sunset Sound, Hollywood

Talkin' To My Heart	TIME
Hollywood (Some Other Kind Of Town)	TIME
Blow By Blow	TIME
Winds Of Change	TIME
I Do	TIME
Nothing Without You	TIME
Dreamin' The Dream	TIME
Sooner Or Later	TIME
I Wonder Why	TIME
Nights In Estoril	TIME
I Got It In For You	TIME
All Over Again	TIME
These Strange Times	TIME

Guitar/Vocals: Billy Burnette
Guitar/Vocals: Dave Mason
Vocals: Bekka Bramlett
Bass: John McVie

Drums/Percussion: Mick Fleetwood
Keyboards/Vocals: Christine McVie
Additional Guitars: Michael Thompson
Additional Keyboards: Steve Thoma
Keyboards: John Jones
Trumpet: Fred Tackett
Additional Background Vocals: Lindsey
 Buckingham/Lucy Fleetwood

Producer: Fleetwood Mac/Richard Dashut
Engineer: Ken Allardyce
Additional Engineering by: Allen Sides/David Eike/
 Tom Nellen/Richard Huredia/Dave Shiffman
Assistant Engineers: Alan Sanderson/Charlie
 Brocco

left *Recent photo of the control room at Sunset Sound.*

above *Mick Fleetwood and Stevie Nicks.*

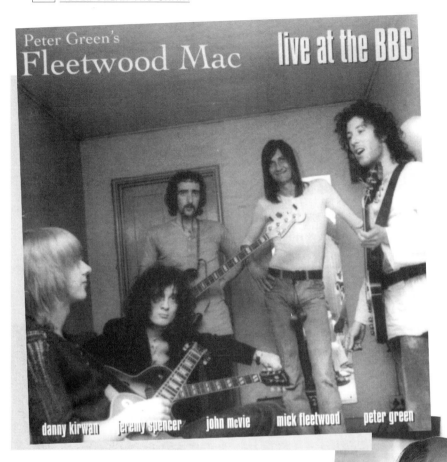

Peter Green's **Fleetwood Mac** live at the BBC

danny kirwan   jeremy spencer   john mcvie   mick fleetwood   peter green

right *CD cover of the* Live at the BBC *album.*

below *Mick Fleetwood at the press launch for the* Live at the BBC *CD.*

After an absence of over a decade, not counting the one-off appearance at President Clinton's Inaugural party, the classic line-up of Fleetwood Mac – Mick Fleetwood, John McVie, Christine McVie, Lindsey Buckingham and Stevie Nicks – reunited and signed with Reprise Records. The plan was to record an unplugged special for MTV and future album release.

LINDSEY BUCKINGHAM: . . . *I hadn't seen Mick Fleetwood for several years. Then one day we got together over breakfast and both Mick and myself were completely different people. So we decided to work on some tracks for my solo album. Originally, we had another bass player but it hadn't worked, so we said, Why don't we get John (McVie) in? Then Christine (McVie) joined us on keyboards. So one day all four of us were sitting in the control room together. We were all having a good time and I think a lightbulb lit up in the*

head of someone at WEA and possibly in Mick's too. We realized we would have to consider making another Fleetwood Mac record and the details were hammered out over the next few months.
(Q Magazine, 1997)

On 18 April Fleetwood Mac held a rehearsal for the upcoming unplugged tapings at Warner's Studios in Burbank, California. Of the material rehearsed on this day several tracks would not make it to the final set list for the show. The performance would include many of their best-known and loved hits along with a selection of new material.

REHEARSALS FOR MTV's 'UNPLUGGED'
Warner Bros Studios, Burbank, California
18 April 1997

The Chain	*Unissued*
Dreams	*Unissued*
Big Love	*Unissued*
Say You Love Me	*Unissued*
Second Hand News	*Unissued*
Where Were You	*Unissued*
Rhiannon	*Unissued*
Little Lies	*Unissued*
Twisted	*Unissued*
Never Going Back Again	*Unissued*
Brown Eyes	*Unissued*
Forbidden	*Unissued*
Shadows Of Love	*Unissued*
Don't Stop	*Unissued*
Go Your Own Way	*Unissued*
Landslide	*Unissued*
Songbird	*Unissued*
Little Lies	*Unissued*

Guitar/Vocals: Lindsey Buckingham
Vocals: Stevie Nicks
Bass: John McVie
Drums: Mick Fleetwood
Keyboards/Vocals: Christine McVie
University of Southern California Trojan
    Marching Band

Producer: —
Engineers: —

MICK FLEETWOOD: *Although there were turbulent times there has been an emotional bond between us. It made the whole process of getting back together happen very organically. We've kept in touch over the years and worked on various projects together. It was all very natural and very comfortable. I know I speak for the rest of the band when I say that this is just another step in an on-going creative collaboration.*
(Warner Brothers Press Release, 1997)

An audience of 800 each night, including a few celebrities: Jacob Dylan, Luke Perry, Courtney Love, Winona Ryder and Brian Wilson, watched a passionate performance by the group. The new songs, especially Buckingham's 'Bleed To Love Her' and Nicks' 'Sweet Girl' were well received.

LIVE SESSIONS FOR MTVs 'UNPLUGGED'
Warner Bros Studios, Burbank, California
22/23 May 1997

The Chain	THE DANCE
Dreams	THE DANCE
Everywhere	THE DANCE
Gold Dust Woman	THE DANCE VIDEO
I'm So Afraid	THE DANCE
Temporary One	THE DANCE
Bleed To Love Her	THE DANCE
Gypsy	THE DANCE VIDEO
Big Love	THE DANCE
Go Insane	THE DANCE VIDEO
Landslide	THE DANCE
Say You Love	THE DANCE
You Make Loving Fun	THE DANCE
My Little Demon	THE DANCE
Silver Springs	A-side/THE DANCE
Over My Head	THE DANCE VIDEO
Rhiannon	THE DANCE
Sweet Girl	THE DANCE
Go Your Own Way	THE DANCE
Tusk	THE DANCE
Don't Stop	THE DANCE
Songbird	THE DANCE VIDEO

Guitar/Vocals: Lindsey Buckingham
Vocals: Stevie Nicks
Bass: John McVie

Fleetwood Mac

Over the last 30 years & 70,000,000 albums the world's been dancing

Congratulations on a truly outstanding contribution to British Music.

'The Dance'- out - now - 21 of their greatest hits
recorded to celebrate the 20th anniversary of 'Rumours'.

wea

Drums: Mick Fleetwood
Keyboards/Vocals: Christine McVie
Keyboards/Guitar/Backing Vocals: Brett Tuggle
Guitar/Backing Vocals: Neale Heywood
Percussion: Lenny Castro
Background Vocals: Sharon Celani
Background Vocals: Mindy Stein
University of Southern California Trojan Marching
   Band ('Tusk' and 'Don't Stop' only)

Producers: Lindsey Buckingham
Engineers: Elliot Scheiner/Barry Goldberg
Additional/Assitant Engineers: Guy Charboneau/
   Charlie Bouis/John Nelson

left *Music press ad celebrating Fleetwood Mac's contribution to British music.*

below *The original* RUMOURS *line-up re-form for the MTV Special.*

The use of the USC Trojan Marching Band enabled Fleetwood Mac to perform the song 'Tusk' as originally recorded.

'Silver Springs' was lifted as a single and received heavy airplay on MTV and VH-1 throughout the Summer and several television appearances helped promote the album.

In September Fleetwood Mac were number one in America on the Top Music Video Charts (THE DANCE), Top Pop Catalog Albums (GREATEST HITS) and Album Chart (THE DANCE).

STEVIE NICKS: *This time 'round, maybe for the first time there's a good feeling between all five of us, and that makes everything okay.*
(Entertainment Weekly, June 6, 1997)

AT THE TIME OF GOING TO PRESS FLEETWOOD MAC HAVE BEEN INDUCTED INTO THE ROCK AND ROLL HALL OF FAME. A FITTING TRIBUTE ON WHICH TO END THIS LOOK BACK AT THEIR MUSIC AND CAREER.

Recording Technology

THIRTY YEARS AGO the recording industry was very different from the computer-controlled mixing desk and digital 48-track facilities we have today. Most artists recorded live with the minimum amount of over-dubbing. This was due to the fact that most bands were live performers who made records as an extension of that art to promote their concerts, rather than being manufactured as recording artists in the studio. The other reason they had to record live was due to the minimal multi-track facilities restricting multiple overdubbing sessions. Only four-track analogue machines were available during this time so that meant only a couple of solo parts recorded on separate tracks could be replaced after the basic track was recorded. The echo and EQ changes were made during the initial recording of the four-track tape so the mix down to stereo was just a simple re-balance of the four tracks. There was, however, the option of editing between different takes to eliminate faulty sections of the original recorded performance.

PETER GREEN'S FLEETWOOD MAC, the first album for Blue Horizon, was recorded this way on to a four-track machine as a complete live performance

Engineer Mike Ross at CBS Studios, London in the late 1960s.

including live vocals with no overdubbing. This four-track master was then mixed down to stereo on to a separate two-track machine known as the final master. The only mix changes that could be made were the balance between the basic rhythm track and solo parts; additional echo and EQ changes could still be made at this stage if required. To save tracks for other instruments the drum kit had to be recorded on one mono track and the stereo positional restrictions of the mix meant that the drum kit ended up on the left or right of the stereo picture. Today's multi-track recordings always feature the drum kit in true stereo. Live recording went some way to minimize this problem as the drum and guitar ambiance in the room would be recorded by the centre-positioned live vocal microphone and this would help pan the drum and guitar ambiance towards the centre of the stereo image. This room ambiance helped to fill up the stereo picture and added to the live feel, which contributed to the sound of Fleetwood Mac's early recordings.

When we came to record the album MR WONDERFUL the band wanted to create the live vocal sound from their concerts, so they decided to set up their own concert PA loudspeaker system in the studio, which they used to amplify their live vocals. We then recorded the vocals direct from the PA loudspeakers using studio microphones. This process gave the vocals an aggressive quality with much more depth and this added to the album's authentic early-American blues sound. In fact there was discussion at the time about pressing this album on a ten-inch disc that could be sold in a brown paper sleeve just like the old original 78 rpm blues records.

Control room at Record Plant in Hollywood.

The control room at CBS Studios in London in the late sixties.

The band started to move away from an all-live recording approach and more into production with the single 'Black Magic Woman'. The basic track was recorded as before but the vocals and guitar parts were overdubbed afterwards, allowing us more control in balancing the final mix. Our mixing approach was much more creative than on earlier recordings as we were able to make guitar panning moves with wild echo effects and vocal echo changes with the added separation.

The next single 'Need Your Love So Bad' was recorded the same way with the addition of a second four-track machine. A two-track mix was made of the rhythm section, vocals and solo guitar from the first four-track machine on to the first two tracks of the second four-track machine which became the second-stage master and, for the first time on a Fleetwood Mac session, a brass and string section were overdubbed on to the remaining two tracks. Our second-stage master now contained the stereo mix of the first-stage master with the brass and string section overdubs. These four tracks were then mixed down to a final stereo tape. By working this way we had the advantage of two extra tracks to record and separate the brass and string section overdubs.

With the single 'Albatross' a new approach was adopted. The band and producer Mike Vernon had just returned from America and had heard a lot of inventive American productions that had been recorded on the new eight-track machines which were available there. The band were very keen to create a new sound, so it was decided to record every instrument separately to achieve perfection. We again used the two four-track machine formula. These machines were not running in sync together as the technology for this function was not available at the time so we were basically only recording four tracks at any single time and mixing at each stage. First we laid down the tom-toms on the first two tracks in stereo, then the rhythm guitar parts and bass guitar on the last two tracks of the first machine. We then made a stereo mix of our first-stage master on to the first two tracks of the second machine, which became our second-stage master, leaving two free tracks to record the lead guitar parts and second rhythm guitar. These four tracks were then mixed down to stereo on two tracks of a new reel of tape on the first four-track machine. This we called our third-stage master. As we were mixing down to our third stage we overdubbed live into this mix the cymbal parts in stereo. We now had two free tracks remaining for the lead guitar harmony part and the echo-answering guitar. Our mixing decisions had to be final at each mix-down stage because we could not go back and re-mix without recording many of the instruments again. Because we were re-balancing and adjusting echo and EQ at each mix-down stage all that was left to add to the final mix were the harmony lead guitar and to our mixed stereo track from the first two tracks of our third-stage master the echo-answering guitar. By working this way we were in effect recording on twelve tracks.

All this track-bouncing, as it was known, was achieved without any noise reduction methods and it is amazing how quiet those early valve microphones and machines were. The tape noise is very low even now when heard on today's CD transfers from the original album tapes. We all felt we had made as near a perfect recording as possible: a true stereo recording with panning tom-toms, cymbals in stereo and the bass guitar in the correct centre position (as opposed to the left or right position which was the usual problem with most four-track stereo recordings).

I have clear memories of a post-session discussion about the possibility of releasing 'Albatross' as a single and whether the release would harm their reputation as a blues band. In England 'Albatross' was released twice, first reaching number one, then number two the second time around, three years later.

This recording marked the end of Fleetwood Mac's association with Blue Horizon and the end of their blues period. They signed up with Reprise Records and went on to worldwide recognition as a rock band and are still making wonderful records today.

I value my experiences of those early days and I feel fortunate to have been involved in their recordings at the beginning.

Mike Ross-Trevor, Recording Engineer
Whitfield Street Studios, London
November 1997

Recording Terminology

1st Stage Master: First recording, usually just the rhythm track.

2nd Stage Master: Mix of the 1st stage master to which subsequent overdubs will be made. Further mixes etc were consecutively numbered, i.e. 3rd stage master etc.

Ambiance: Reverberation characteristics of a room.

Backing Track: Pre-recorded track on which vocals and other instruments are overdubbed.

Basic Track: Same as backing track.

Bouncing: A process used in multi-track recording, involving mixing and bouncing tracks onto a single track.

Edit: Process of splicing tape to improve a performance.

EQ (Equalisation): Changing the frequency to alter the sound, usually at the mixing stage.

False Start: An incomplete take often caused by the artist or musician singing or playing a wrong note.

Four-track: A tape or tape machine with four separate tracks.

Master: Version/take finally chosen for release.

Mono Remix: Remix down from multiple track to a single track.

Out-takes: Other versions of a song not used as the master.

Overdub: The process of adding extra vocals and/or instruments to an already existing track.

Panning: Physical positioning of a sound, left or right, in a stereo picture.

Re-make: Another attempt at recording a particular track.

Reverberation: Degree of ambience in a room.

Session tape: Original tape as recorded at the session.

Stereo Remix: Reduction from a multi-track tape down to a stereo master.

Two-track: A tape having two independent tracks.

Fleetwood Mac Biographies

I N THE RELATIVELY short time-span of 30 years there have been many different incarnations of Fleetwood Mac. Many only lasted a few months while others, the Buckingham/Nicks period for example, spanned 12 years and spawned five enormously successful albums. This section gives brief biographies of all the members of Fleetwood Mac past and present detailing their careers before, during and after their spell in the group. Throughout their illustrious careers the two founder members, Mick Fleetwood and John McVie, have been the mainstay of the group while other individual members have each brought their own style and songwriting skill to the group.

MICK FLEETWOOD

M ICK FLEETWOOD was born on 24 June 1947 in Redruth. At the age of 13 his father bought him his first drum kit. He taught himself to play by listening to records by The Everly Brothers and Cliff Richard and the Shadows, and as time moved on he became obsessed with drumming. His drumming came to the attention of Peter Barden who invited him to join his group The Cheynes, one of the first groups to jump on the R & B bandwagon. This was mid-1963 and around the time he first met up with John McVie. The group disbanded in 1965 and he spent a few months drumming with the Bo Street Runners, appearing on just one single, before Peter Barden recruited him once again for his new band Peter B's Looners, later to become Peter B's. It was here that he made friends with a talented guitarist by the name of Peter Green. The addition of two new members, Rod Stewart and Beryl Marsden, and a name change to Shotgun Express, only lasted a few months before Mick Fleetwood moved onto the Bluesbreakers. Although he was only in the band for a few months it strengthened the relationship between Fleetwood, McVie and Green. A founder member of Fleetwood Mac, he has seen the group through a number of ups and downs, as well as many line-ups and successes. His first solo album was THE VISITOR in 1981 and with his group The Zoo, he released I'M NOT ME in 1983 and SHAKIN' THE CAGE in 1992.

JOHN McVIE

JOHN McVIE was born in Ealing, West London on 26 November 1945 and turned his attentions towards playing the guitar at the age of 14. A friend of McVie's gave John Mayall, who was looking for a bassist for his newly formed group the Bluesbreakers, his telephone number and McVie subsequently became a member of this famed blues outfit. It was Mayall who taught McVie the rudiments of the blues. He was in the Bluesbreakers for nearly five years, although he was fired several times for excessive drinking but was always re-hired. When Mick Fleetwood and Peter Green joined the band the roots of a new group were formed, and they later departed and formed Fleetwood Mac. It was McVie that Green intended to be the 'Mac' in the group. With its financial security, McVie was loathe to leave the Bluesbreakers but in September 1967 he finally became a member of Fleetwood Mac and is still with the group to this day. He has appeared on all their albums and in 1971 he was responsible for the adoption of the Penguin logo that the band has used ever since. He was the last member of the group to release a solo album, JOHN McVIE'S "GOTTA BAND" WITH LOLA THOMAS, released in 1992.

PETER GREEN

PETER ALLEN GREENBAUM was born in London's East End on 29 October 1946 and first became interested in music at the age of ten, when his brother brought home a cheap Spanish guitar. His early influences included Hank Marvin and Muddy Waters and by the time he was 15 he was playing in local groups, having changed his name to Peter Green. In 1965 he joined The Muskrats and got his first taste of R & B music. His spell with the group came to an end in November when he was invited by Peter Barden to join his group Peter B's Looners. It was here that he made his recording debut on the single 'If You Wanna Be Happy'. This was to be another short-lived acquaintance when, in May 1966, he moved on to Shotgun Express. This line-up recorded two unsuccessful singles and then it was time to move on. His invitation to join John Mayall's Bluesbreakers was an offer he could not refuse. Eric Clapton had left the Bluesbreakers and Peter was an obvious choice as his replacement. It was during his spell with Mayall that his friendship with Mick Fleetwood and John McVie developed. It was prophetic that while with Mayall they recorded an instrumental titled 'Fleetwood Mac'. After a string of successful albums and singles Green was faced with the problem of handling the wealth and fame that came with being a rock star and finally quit the band in May 1970. Since leaving the band he has released several solo efforts, not always successfully. His first, END OF THE GAME, failed to capture any of the Peter Green magic but subsequent albums, IN THE SKIES, LITTLE DREAMER, WATCHA GONNA DO, BLUE GUITAR, WHITE SKY, KOLORS and COME ON DOWN have seen a gradual return to form. He recently recorded and toured with his new group Splinter.

BOB BRUNNING

THE ORIGINAL bass player in the group, Bob Brunning, left in September 1967 and formed the Brunning Hall Sunflower Blues Band recording several albums, BULLEN STREET BLUES, TRACKSIDE BLUES and I WISH YOU WOULD. As a member of the De Luxe Blues Band he has appeared on A STREET CAR NAMED DE-LUXE, LIVE AT HALF MOON PUTNEY, URBAN DE-LUXE and MOTORVATING. Bob has additionally recorded another twenty or so albums since his stint with Fleetwood Mac, combining this with his work as a London head-teacher. Recently retired, he is writing a series of books about music for children, runs a blues club and still plays with the De Luxe Blues Band, who recently recorded their seventh CD. His newly updated biography of Fleetwood Mac was published in 1998.

JEREMY SPENCER

A MEMBER OF the Birmingham-based Levi Set from November 1966 until June 1967 Spencer was a lover of both the blues, especially Elmore James, and also Elvis Presley and couldn't make up his mind what direction to take. Spotted by Mike Vernon, who was impressed by his slide-guitar playing, he joined Fleetwood Mac in July 1967 and appeared on PETER GREEN'S FLEETWOOD MAC, MR WONDERFUL, and KILN HOUSE. During their American tour in 1971 Spencer disappeared and joined The Children Of God. His recording career did not end there, for he released several albums – JEREMY SPENCER, JEREMY SPENCER AND THE CHILDREN OF GOD and FLEE. During his time with Fleetwood Mac he contributed several songs and often had the chance, on stage, to demonstrate his love of rock 'n' roll, performing several classic songs from the fifties.

DANNY KIRWAN

ORIGINALLY IN Boilerhouse, Danny Kirwan joined Fleetwood Mac in August 1968. It was Mike Vernon who recommended Kirwan to the group. During his time with them he appeared on THEN PLAY ON, KILN HOUSE, FUTURE GAMES and BARE TREES. In August 1972 he left the group and throughout the seventies recorded several albums for the DJM label including SECOND CHAPTER, MIDNIGHT IN SAN JUAN and HELLO THERE BIG BOY.

CHRISTINE McVIE

CHRISTINE McVIE'S first band was an R & B outfit from the West Midlands, Shades Of Blue, of which she was a member for just a year from March 1964, before returning to college. In 1967, at the invite of ex-Shades Of Blue members Andy Sylvester and Stan Webb, she joined Chicken Shack on keyboards and played at the Windsor Festival, along with Fleetwood Mac. Both groups would often run into each other while playing the same round of clubs and it was during this time she met John McVie.

In 1969 she decided to quit the music business, just as Chicken Shack's 'I'd Rather Go Blind' was released and she was voted Best Female Vocalist by Melody Maker. A brief spell with her own band the Christine Perfect Band, during which time she released the self-titled album CHRISTINE PERFECT, led to her joining Fleetwood Mac in late 1970. She had previously worked with the band, albeit uncredited, on KILN HOUSE and even painted the cover so when she was asked to join she already knew most of their material. Another prolific songwriter, she made contributions to all their albums from 1971 onwards. In 1984 she felt the time was right to record her solo album, CHRISTINE McVIE. The album produced two memorable singles 'Love Will Show Us How' and 'Got A Hold On Me'.

BOB WELCH

BOB WELCH'S first band was Ivory Hudson & The Harleyquins, later revamped as The Seven Souls, and in 1968 three of the members, including Welch, formed Head West and released the album HEADWEST FEATURING BOB WELCH. In 1971 the group disbanded and Bob Welch joined Fleetwood Mac in the April of that year. He appeared on five albums FUTURE GAMES, BARE TREES, PENGUIN, MYSTERY TO ME and HEROES ARE HARD TO FIND before leaving the group in December 1974. A short spell in the group Paris was followed by a successful solo career that saw him release a number of albums, most notably FRENCH KISS, which went platinum.

DAVE WALKER

DAVE WALKER, hired by the band in 1972 after Danny Kirwan's departure, had previously been the lead singer in Savoy Brown Blues Band appearing on STREET CORNER, HELLBOUND TRAIL and LIONS SHARE. He appeared on just one album during his time with Fleetwood Mac, PENGUIN, and played with them during their late 1972 US tour. In 1973, after it was decided he didn't fit in, he was asked to leave the group.

BOB WESTON

BOB WESTON, like Dave Walker, was brought in to fill the gap left by Danny Kirwan's departure. Born in England he had worked with several groups including Black Cat Bones, appearing on their 1970 album BARBED WIRE SANDWICH, and Ashkan's IN FROM THE COLD. During his brief spell with Fleetwood Mac he appeared on PENGUIN and MYSTERY TO ME. He left the group in October 1973 after personal problems within the group.

LINDSEY BUCKINGHAM

LINDSEY BUCKINGHAM was born in October 1949 in Atherton, California and joined his first band, Fritz, in 1967 leaving in October 1971 to form Buckingham Nicks with another member of Fritz, Stevie Nicks. A deal with Polydor saw the release of the album BUCKINGHAM NICKS in 1973 but unfortunately the album was a non-starter, except in the Birmingham, Alabama area where they seemed to have a cult following. In January 1975 Lindsey was approached by Mick Fleetwood to join Fleetwood Mac, after Fleetwood had heard a tape of one of their songs during a search for a new studio. His first album as a member of the group was FLEETWOOD MAC and he worked on all their albums up to and including TANGO IN THE NIGHT in 1987. After the recording of the album he decided he'd had enough and left to pursue a solo career, although his first solo effort, LAW AND ORDER, had been released in 1981 while he was still with the group. The album produced three singles: 'Trouble', 'The Visitor' and 'Mary Lee Jones' and he followed this with more solo albums including GO INSANE and OUT OF THE CRADLE. Buckingham made a special appearance with Fleetwood Mac at President Clinton's Inaugural Gala in January 1993 and recorded the successful THE DANCE album as part of the original RUMOURS line-up.

STEVIE NICKS

STEVIE NICKS' route to Fleetwood Mac followed the same path as Lindsey Buckingham's – a member of Fritz, then Buckingham Nicks – and she became the most prolific songwriter in the group. Born in May 1948, her love of fairytales and fantasy had been instilled in her by her mother. She worked on all the group's albums from FLEETWOOD MAC in 1975 to BEHIND THE MASK in 1990. Like Lindsey Buckingham she made an appearance with the group at President Clinton's Inaugural Gala in January 1993 and the subsequent recording of THE DANCE. During her time with the group she released several solo albums – BELLA DONNA, THE WILD HEART, ROCK A LITTLE and THE OTHER SIDE OF THE MIRROR. Her fifth solo album, STREET ANGEL, and a best of set TIMESPACE were released after her departure from the group.

BILLY BURNETTE

THE SON OF fifties rocker Dorsey Burnette, Billy was born in Memphis on 8 May 1953 and first recorded at the tender age of nine when he sang a duet with his dad. Along with his cousin Rocky he often appeared as the Dorsey Brothers Show playing the local clubs. He joined Fleetwood Mac at the same time as Rick Vito and worked on the BEHIND THE MASK and TIME albums. Before joining he had worked on Mick Fleetwood's Zoo album, I'M NOT ME, and released a number of solo albums including BETWEEN FRIENDS, GIMME YOU and SOLDIER OF LOVE. He recently released an album with Bekka Bramlett.

RICK VITO

RICK VITO, a native Philadelphian, had seen Fleetwood Mac live back in 1968 and had been influenced by Peter Green. After a brief spell with John Mayall in the mid-seventies, during which time he appeared on NEW YEAR, NEW BAND, NEW COMPANY and NOTICE TO APPEAR, Vito worked on sessions for Bob Seger, Bonnie Raitt, Maria Muldaur and Jackson Browne. He joined Fleetwood Mac in 1987, after Lindsey Buckingham's departure, and toured with the group during the TANGO IN THE NIGHT tour. He can be heard on the 1990 album BEHIND THE MASK. After leaving the band in 1993 he released a solo album, KING OF HEARTS.

BEKKA BRAMLETT

BEKKA BRAMLETT, the daughter of white rock/soul duo Delaney & Bonnie, was born on 1 April 1968 and joined Fleetwood Mac in March 1994. She appeared on the 1995 album TIME and after touring with the group left the band in 1996. Bekka had previously worked with Mick Fleetwood's band The Zoo on the 1992 album SHAKIN' THE CAGE. Recently she worked with Billy Burnette on a joint album project.

DAVE MASON

DAVE MASON, an ex-Spencer Davis Group roadie was born 10 May 1947 and his first group, Traffic, formed with Steve Winwood, Chris Wood and Jim Capaldi, had hits with 'Paper Sun', 'Hole In My Shoe' (written by Mason) and 'Here We Go Round The Mulberry Bush'. He left the group in December 1967 only to re-join in May the following year. After he quit for the second time in October 1968 Mason began a solo career that would see him release several albums, including DAVE MASON AND CASS ELLIOT, HEADKEEPER, DAVE MASON IS ALIVE! and SPLIT COCONUT. He joined Fleetwood Mac in 1994 at the same time as Bekka Bramlett. Interestingly he had previously worked with Delaney & Bonnie & Friends back in 1970.

Complete Discography

THE FOLLOWING discography details all the group's singles, UK and US issues with their various formats and albums. It is followed by a complete list of videos and selected bootlegs. In all cases only the first issue is listed, although many were re-issued in different covers and combinations, and often featured different artwork to the originals. Most of the material is now available on compact disc. The final section of this discography gives an insight to the volume of work the various members of Fleetwood Mac undertook as solo artists, either before, during or after their spell with the group. The albums listed in this section only detail the title, catalogue number and release dates.

SINGLES

I BELIEVE MY TIME AIN'T LONG/RAMBLING PONY

(UK) Blue Horizon 57-3051
3 November 1967

BLACK MAGIC WOMAN/WHEN THE SUN IS SHINING

(UK) Blue Horizon 57-3138
29 March 1968

BLACK MAGIC WOMAN/LONG GREY MARE

(US) Epic 5-10351
7 June 1968

NEED YOUR LOVE SO BAD/STOP MESSIN' ROUND

(UK) Blue Horizon 57-3139
5 July 1968

ALBATROSS/JIGSAW PUZZLE BLUES

(UK) Blue Horizon 57-3145
22 November 1968

ALBATROSS/JIGSAW PUZZLE BLUES

(US) Epic 5-10436
1 January 1969

MAN OF THE WORLD/SOMEBODY'S GONNA GET THEIR HEAD KICKED IN TONIGHT

(UK) Immediate IM 080
April 1969

RATTLESNAKE SHAKE/COMING YOUR WAY

(US) Reprise 0860
September 1969

OH WELL (Part 1)/OH WELL (Part 2)

(UK) Reprise RS 27000
26 September 1969

OH WELL (Part 1)/OH WELL (Part 2)

(US) Reprise REP 0883
19 November 1969

THE GREEN MANALISHI (WITH THE TWO-PRONG CROWN)/WORLD IN HARMONY

(UK) Reprise RS 27007
15 May 1970

THE GREEN MANALISHI (WITH THE TWO-PRONG CROWN)/WORLD IN HARMONY

(US) Reprise REP 0925
3 June 1970

JEWEL EYED JUDY/STATION MAN

(US) Reprise REP 0984
January 1971

DRAGONFLY/THE PURPLE DANCER

(US) Reprise RS 27010
March 1971

SANDS OF TIME/LAY IT ALL DOWN

(US) Reprise REP 1057
10 November 1971

SENTIMENTAL LADY/SUNNY SIDE OF HEAVEN

(US) Reprise REP 1093
May 1972

SPARE ME A LITTLE/SUNNY SIDE OF HEAVEN

(UK) Reprise K 14194
August 1972

REMEMBER ME/DISSATISFIED

(US) Reprise REP 1159
16 May 1973

DID YOU EVER LOVE ME/THE DERELICT

(UK) Reprise K 14280
22 June 1973

DID YOU EVER LOVE ME/REVELATION

(US) Reprise REP 1172
29 August 1973

FOR YOUR LOVE/HYPNOTIZED

(US) Reprise REP 1188
12 December 1973

FOR YOUR LOVE/HYPNOTIZED

(UK) Reprise K 14315
8 March 1974

HEROES ARE HARD TO FIND/BORN ENCHANTER

(US) Reprise RSP 1317
September 1974

HEROES ARE HARD TO FIND/BORN ENCHANTER

(UK) Reprise K 14388
February 1975

OVER MY HEAD (Edit)/I'M SO AFRAID

(US) Reprise RPS 1339
24 September 1975

WARM WAYS/ BLUE LETTER

(UK) Reprise K 14403
24 October 1975

OVER MY HEAD *(Edit)*/**I'M SO AFRAID**

(UK) Reprise K 14413
13 February 1976

RHIANNON/SUGAR DADDY

(US) Reprise RPS 1345
January 1976

RHIANNON/SUGAR DADDY

(UK) Reprise K 14430
April 1976

SAY YOU LOVE ME/MONDAY MORNING

(US) Reprise RPS 1356
9 June 1976

SAY YOU LOVE ME/MONDAY MORNING

(UK) Reprise K 14447
24 September 1976

GO YOUR OWN WAY/SILVER SPRINGS

(US) Warner Brothers WBS 8304
20 December 1976

GO YOUR OWN WAY/SILVER SPRINGS

(UK) Warner Brothers K 16872
28 January 1977

DON'T STOP/GOLD DUST WOMAN

(UK) Warner Brothers K 16930
1 April 1977

DREAMS/SONGBIRD

(US) Warner Brothers WBS 8371
4 April 1977

DON'T STOP/NEVER GOING BACK AGAIN

(US) Warner Brothers WBS 8413
6 July 1977

DREAMS/SONGBIRD

(UK) Warner Brothers K 16969
17 June 1977

**YOU MAKE LOVING FUN/NEVER GOING
 BACK AGAIN**

(UK) Warner Brothers K 17013
16 September 1977

**YOU MAKE LOVING FUN/GOLD DUST
 WOMAN**

(US) Warner Brothers WBS 8483
5 October 1977

TUSK/NEVER MAKE ME CRY

(UK) Warner Brothers K 17468
September 1979

TUSK/NEVER MAKE ME CRY

(US) Warner Brothers WBS 49077
October 1979

SARA/THAT'S ENOUGH FOR ME

(UK) Warner Brothers K 17533
December 1979

SARA/THAT'S ENOUGH FOR ME

(US) Warner Brothers WBS 49150
December 1979

NOT THAT FUNNY/SAVE ME A PLACE

(UK) Warner Brothers K 17577
February 1980

THINK ABOUT ME/SAVE ME A PLACE

(US) Warner Brothers WBS 49196
March 1980

THINK ABOUT ME/HONEY HI

(UK) Warner Brothers K 17614
May 1980

SISTERS OF THE MOON/WALK A THIN LINE

(US) Warner Brothers WBS 49500
May 1980

THE FARMER'S DAUGHTER *(Live)*/**DREAMS**
 (Live)

(UK) Warner Brothers K 17746
February 1981

FIREFLIES *(Live)*/**OVER MY HEAD** *(Live)*

(US)Warner Brothers WBS 49660
February 1981

THE FARMER'S DAUGHTER *(Live)*/**MONDAY
 MORNING** *(Live)*

(US) Warner Brothers WB 49700
March 1981

HOLD ME/EYES OF THE WORLD

(US) Warner Brothers WBS 29966
June 1982

HOLD ME/EYES OF THE WORLD

(UK) Warner Brothers K 17965
July 1982

GYPSY (Edit)/COOL WATER

(UK) Warner Brothers K 17997
September 1982

GYPSY (Edit)/COOL WATER

(US) Warner Brothers WBS 29918
September 1982

LOVE IN STORE/CAN'T GO BACK

(US) Warner Brothers WBS 29918
November 1982

OH DIANE/ONLY OVER YOU

(UK) Warner Brothers FLEET 1
(UK) Warner Brothers FLEET 1P (Picture Disc)
(UK) Warner Brothers FLEET 1T (12in with
bonus track The Chain)
December 1982

OH DIANE/THAT'S ALRIGHT

(US) Warner Brothers 7-29698
March 1983

CAN'T GO BACK/THAT'S ALRIGHT

(UK) Warner Brothers W 9848
(UK) Warner Brothers W 9848T (12in with
alternate B-side Rhiannon and bonus tracks
Tusk and Over And Over)
April 1983

BIG LOVE/YOU AND I, Part 1

(UK) Warner Brothers W 8398
(UK) Warner Brothers W 8398F (double-pack
with bonus tracks The Chain and Go Your
Own Way)
(UK) Warner Brothers W 8398T (12in with
Big Love (Extended version))

(UK) Warner Brothers W 8398TP (12in
picture disc with Big Love (Extended
version))
April 1987

BIG LOVE/YOU AND I, Part 1

(US) Warner Brothers W 28398
(US) Warner Brothers W 0-20683 (12in with
Big Love (Extended mix) and bonus tracks
Big Love (House on the Hill dub) and Big
Love (Piano dub))
April 1987

SEVEN WONDERS/BOOK OF MIRACLES
(Instrumental)

(UK) Warner Brothers W 8317
(UK)Warner Brothers W 8317T (12in with
bonus track Seven Wonders (Extended remix)
and Seven Wonders (Dub))
(UK) Warner Brothers W 8317TP (12in
picture disc with same tracks as W 8317T)
June 1987

SEVEN WONDERS/BOOK OF MIRACLES
(Instrumental)

(US) Warner Brothers 28317
(US) Warner Brothers 20739 (12in with
bonus track Seven Wonders (Extended remix)
and Seven Wonders (Dub))
June 1987

LITTLE LIES (Single version)/RICKY

(US) Warner Brothers 28291
(US) Warner Brothers (12in with bonus track
Little Lies (Extended) and Little Lies (Dub))
August 1987

LITTLE LIES (Single version)/RICKY

(UK) Warner Brothers W 8291
(UK) Warner Brothers W 8291T (12in with
bonus track Little Lies (Extended) and
Little Lies (Dub))
(UK) Warner Brothers W 8291TP (12in
picture disc with same tracks as W 8291T)
(UK) Warner Brothers W 8291C (cassette
with same tracks as W 8291T)
September 1987

FAMILY MAN/DOWN ENDLESS STREET

(UK) Warner Brothers W 8114
(UK) Warner Brothers W 8114B (box set
with 2 prints and different B-side You And I,
Part II)
(UK) Warner Brothers W 8114T (12in
featuring Family Man (*Extended vocal remix*),
Family Party (*Bonus Beats*) and You And I,
Part II)
September 1987

EVERYWHERE/WHEN I SEE YOU AGAIN

(US) Warner Brothers 28143
(US) Warner Brothers 4-28143 (Cassette
single with same tracks as 28143)
November 1987

EVERYWHERE/WHEN I SEE YOU AGAIN

(UK) Warner Brothers W 8143
(UK) Warner Brothers W 8143T (12in
with bonus tracks Everywhere (*Extended
version*) and Everywhere (*Dub version*))
(UK) Warner Brothers W 8143CD (3in CD
single with bonus tracks Rhiannon and Say
You Love Me)
March 1988

FAMILY MAN/YOU AND I, Part II

(US) Warner Brothers 28114
(US) Warner Brothers 0-2084 (12in
featuring Family Man (*Extended vocal remix*),
Family Man (*I'm a Jazz Man dub mix*),
Family Man (*Extended guitar remix*) Family
Party (*Bonus beats*) and Down Endless
Street)
(US) Warner Brothers 4-28114 (Cassette
single with same tracks as 28114)
September 1987

ISN'T IT MIDNIGHT/MYSTIFIED

(UK) Warner Brothers W 7860
(UK) Warner Brothers W 7860T (12in with
bonus tracks Say You Love Me and Gypsy)
(UK) Warner Brothers W 7860CD (3in CD
single with same tracks as W 7860T)
June 1988

AS LONG AS YOU FOLLOW/OH WELL (*Live*)

(US) Warner Brothers 7-27644
(US) Warner Brothers 2-27644 (CD single
with same tracks as W 7644T)
(US) Warner Brothers 4-27644 (Cassette
single with same tracks as 7-27644)
November 1988

AS LONG AS YOU FOLLOW/OH WELL (*Live*)

(UK) Warner Brothers W 7644
(UK) Warner Brothers W 7644T (12in with
bonus tracks Gold Dust Woman)
(UK) Warner Brothers W 7644CD (3in CD
single with same tracks as W 7644T)
(UK) Warner Brothers W 7644C (Cassette
single with same tracks as W 7644)
December 1988

HOLD ME/NO QUESTIONS ASKED

(UK) Warner Brothers W 7528
(UK) Warner Brothers W 7528T (12in
single with bonus track I Loved Another
Woman (*Live*))
(UK) Warner Brothers W 7528CD (3in CD
single with same tracks as W 7528T)
February 1989

SAVE ME/ANOTHER WOMAN (*Live*)

(US) Warner Brothers 7-019866
(US) Warner Brothers 4-019866 (Cassette
single with same title both sides)
March 1990

SAVE ME/ANOTHER WOMAN (*Live*)

(UK) Warner Brothers W 9866
(UK) Warner Brothers W 9866C (Cassette
single with same tracks as W 9866)
(UK) Warner Brothers W 9866T (12in
single with bonus track Everywhere
(*Live*))
(UK) Warner Brothers W 9866CD (CD
single with same tracks as W 9866T)
(UK) Warner Brothers W 9866CDX
(CD collectors edition with fold out sleeve
and same tracks as W 9866T)
April 1990

SKIES THE LIMIT/LIZARD PEOPLE

(US) Warner Brothers 7-019867
(US) Warner Brothers 4-019867 (Cassette single with same tracks as 7-019867)
July 1990

IN THE BACK OF MY MIND *(Edit)*/LIZARD PEOPLE

(UK) Warner Brothers W 9739
(UK) Warner Brothers W 9739C (Cassette single with same tracks as W 9739)
(UK) Warner Brothers W 9739T (12in single with different B-side Little Lies (*Live*) and bonus track The Chain (*Live*))
(UK) Warner Brothers W 9739CD (CD single with same tracks as W 9739T)
(UK) Warner Brothers W 9739CDX (CD collectors edition with fold-out sleeve with same tracks as W 9739CD plus Lizard People)
August 1990

HARD FEELINGS/FREEDOM

(US) Warner Brothers 4-19537
October 1990

SKIES THE LIMIT/LIZARD PEOPLE

(UK) Warner Brothers W 9740
(UK) Warner Brothers W 9740C (Cassette single with same tracks as W 9740)
(UK) Warner Brothers W 9740T (12in single with different B-side Little Lies (*Live*) and bonus track The Chain (*Live*))
(UK) Warner Brothers W 9740CD (CD single with same tracks as W 9740T)
November 1990

LOVE SHINES *(Album Version)*/THE CHAIN *(Alternate Mix)*

(UK) Warner Brothers W 0145
(UK) Warner Brothers W 0145C (Cassette single with same tracks as W 0145)
(UK) Warner Brothers W 0145T (12in single with bonus tracks The Chain (*Not That Funny live version*) and Isn't It Midnight (*Edited alternate version*))

Warner Brothers W 0145CD (CD single with same tracks as W 0145T)
January 1993

ALBUMS

PETER GREEN'S FLEETWOOD MAC

Blue Horizon (S) 7-63200
24 February 1968
My Heart Beat Like A Hammer/Merry Go Round/Long Grey Mare/Hellhound On My Trail/Shake Your Moneymaker/Looking For Somebody/No Place To Go/My Baby's Good To Me/I Loved Another Woman/Cold Black Night/The World Keep On Turning/Got To Move

MR WONDERFUL

Blue Horizon 7-63205
23 August 1968
Stop Messin' Round/I've Lost My Baby/Rollin' Man/Dust My Broom/Love That Burns/Doctor Brown/Need Your Love Tonight/If You Be My Baby/Evenin' Boogie/Lazy Poker Blues/Coming Home/Trying So Hard To Forget

ENGLISH ROSE

Epic BN 26446 (US release only)
January 1969
Stop Messin' Round/Jigsaw Puzzle Blues/Doctor Brown/Something Inside Of Me/Evenin' Boogie/Love That Burns/Black Magic Woman/I've Lost My Baby/One Sunny Day/Without You/Coming Home/Albatross

PIOUS BIRD OF GOOD OMEN

Blue Horizon 7-63215
1969
Need Your Love So Bad/Coming Home/Rambling Pony/The Big Boat/I Believe My Time Ain't Long/The Sun Is Shining/Albatross/Black Magic Woman/Just The Blues/Jigsaw Puzzle Blues/Looking For Somebody/Stop Messin' Round

THEN PLAY ON

Reprise RSLP 9000
September 1969
Coming Your Way/Closing My Eyes/Fighting For Madge/When You Say/Show-Biz Blues/Under Way/One Sunny Day/Although The Sun Is Shining/Rattlesnake Shake/Without You/Searching For Madge/My Dream/Like Crying/Before The Beginning

BLUES JAM AT CHESS

Blue Horizon 7-66227
5 December 1969
Watch Out/Ooh Baby/South Indiana-Take 1/South Indiana-Take 2/Last Night/Red Hot Jam/I'm Worried/I Held My Baby Last Night/Madison Blues/I Can't Hold Out/I Need Your Love/I Got The Blues/World's In A Tangle/Talk With You/Like It This Way/Someday Soon Baby/Hungry Country Girl/Black Jack Blues/Everyday I Have The Blues/Rockin' Boogie/Sugar Mama/Homework

KILN HOUSE

Reprise RSLP 9004
18 September 1970
This Is The Rock/Station Man/Blood On The Floor/Hi Ho Silver/Jewel Eyed Judy/Buddy's Song/Earl Gray/One Together/Tell Me All The Things You Do/Mission Bell

THE ORIGINAL FLEETWOOD MAC

CBS 63875
14 May 1971
Driftin'/Leaving Town Blues/Watch Out/A Fool No More/Mean Old Fireman/Can't Afford To Do It/Fleetwood Mac/Worried Dream/Love That Woman/Allow Me One More Show/First Train Home/Rambling Pony #2

BLACK MAGIC WOMAN

Epic EG 30632 (US release only)
25 August 1971
My Heart Beat Like A Hammer/Merry Go Round/Long Grey Mare/Hellhound On My Trail/Shake Your Moneymaker/Looking For Somebody/No Place To Go/My Baby's Good To Me/I Loved Another Woman/Cold Black Night/The World Keep On Turning/Got To Move/Stop Messin' Round/Jigsaw Puzzle Blues/Doctor Brown/Something Inside Of Me/Evenin' Boogie/Love That Burns/Black Magic Woman/I've Lost My Baby/One Sunny Day/Without You/Coming Home/Albatross

FUTURE GAMES

Reprise K 44153
3 September 1971
Woman Of 1000 Years/Morning Rain/What A Shame/Future Games/Sands Of Time/Sometimes/Lay It All Down/Show Me A Smile

FLEETWOOD MAC GREATEST HITS

CBS 69011
November 1971
The Green Manalishi (With The Two Prong Crown)/Oh Well (Part 1)/Oh Well (Part 2)/Shake Your Moneymaker/Dragonfly/Black Magic Woman/Albatross/Man Of The World/Stop Messin' Round/Love That Burns

BARE TREES

Reprise K 44181
July 1972
Child Of Mine/The Ghost/Homeward Bound/Sunny Side Of Heaven/Bare Trees/Sentimental Lady/Danny's Chant/Spare Me A Little Of Your Love/Dust/Thoughts On A Grey Day

PENGUIN

Reprise K 44235
25 May 1973
Remember Me/Bright Fire/Dissatisfied/(I'm A) Road Runner/The Derelict/Revelation/Did You Ever Love Me/Night Watch/Caught In The Rain

MYSTERY TO ME

Reprise K 44248
11 January 1974
Emerald Eyes/Believe Me/Just Crazy Love/Hypnotized/Forever/Keep On Going/The

City/Miles Away/Somebody/The Way I Feel/
For Your Love/Why

HEROES ARE HARD TO FIND

Reprise K 54026
13 September 1974
Heroes Are Hard To Find/Coming Home/
Angel/Bermuda Triangle/Come A Little Bit
Closer/She's Changing Me/Bad Loser/Silver
Heels/Prove Your Love/Born Enchanter/
Safe Harbour

FLEETWOOD MAC

Reprise K 54043
August 1975
Monday Morning/Warm Ways/Blue Letter/
Rhiannon/Over My Head/Crystal/Say You
Love Me/Landslide/World Turning/Sugar
Daddy/I'm So Afraid

RUMOURS

Warner Brothers K 56344
4 February 1977
Second Hand News/Dreams/Never Going
Back Again/Don't Stop/Go Your Own Way/
Songbird/The Chain/You Make Loving Fun/
I Don't Want To Know/Oh Daddy/Gold Dust
Woman

TUSK

Warner Brothers K 66088
October 1979
Over & Over/The Ledge/Think About
Me/Save Me A Place/Sara/What Makes You
Think You're The One/Storms/That's All For
Everyone/Not That Funny/Sisters Of The
Moon/Angel/That's Enough For Me/Brown
Eyes/Never Make Me Cry/I Know I'm Not
Wrong/Honey Hi/Beautiful Child/Walk A
Thin Line/Tusk/Never Forget

FLEETWOOD MAC LIVE

Warner Brothers K 66097
November 1980
Monday Morning/Say You Love
Me/Dreams/Oh Well/Over & Over/Sara/Not
That Funny/Never Going Back Again/

Landslide/Fireflies/Over My Head/Rhiannon/
Don't Let Me Down Again/One More Night/
Go Your Own Way/Don't Stop/I'm So Afraid/
The Farmer's Daughter

MIRAGE

Warner Brothers K 56952
July 1982
Love In Store/Can't Go Back/That's Alright/
Book Of Love/Gypsy/Only Over You/Empire
State/Straight Back/Hold Me/Oh Diane/Eyes
Of The World/Wish You Were Here

TANGO IN THE NIGHT

Warner Brothers WX 65
April 1987
Big Love/Seven Wonders/Everywhere/
Caroline/Tango In The Night/Mystified/Little
Lies/Family Man/Welcome To The Room . . .
Sara/Isn't It Midnight/When I See You Again

GREATEST HITS

Warner Brothers WX 221
November 1988
Rhiannon/Go Your Own Way/Don't Stop/
Gypsy/Everywhere/You Make Loving Fun/Big
Love/As Long As You Follow/Say You Love
Me/Dreams/Little Lies/Oh Diane/Sara/Tusk/
Seven Wonders/Hold Me/No Questions Asked

BEHIND THE MASK

Warner Brothers WX 335
April 1990
Skies The Limit/Love Is Dangerous/In The
Back Of My Mind/Do You Know/Save Me/
Affairs Of The Heart/When The Sun Goes
Down/Behind The Mask/Stand On The Rock/
Hard Feelings/Freedom/When It Comes To
Love/The Second Time

25 YEARS – THE CHAIN

Warner Brothers
1992
Paper Doll/Love Shines/Stand Back (live)/
Crystal/Isn't It Midnight/Big Love/
Everywhere/Affairs Of The Heart/Heart Of
Stone/Sara/That's All For Everyone/Over My

Head/Little Lies/Eyes Of The World/Oh Diane/In The Back Of My Mind/Make Me A Mask/Save Me/Goodbye Angel/Silver Springs/ What Makes You Think You're The One/ Think About Me/Gypsy/You Make Loving Fun/Second Hand News/Love In Store/The Chain/Teen Beat/Dreams/Only Over You/I'm So Afraid/Love Is Dangerous/Gold Dust Woman/Not That Funny (live)/Warm Ways/ Say You Love Me/Don't Stop/Rhiannon/Walk A Thin Line/Storms/Go Your Own Way/ Sisters Of The Moon/Monday Morning/ Landslide/Hypnotized/Lay It All Down/ Angel/Beautiful Child/Brown Eyes/Save Me A Place/Tusk/Never Going Back Again/ Songbird/I Believe My Time Ain't Long/Need Your Love So Bad/Rattlesnake Shake/Oh Well (part 1)/Stop Messin' Round/Green Manalishi/Albatross/Man Of The World/Love That Burns/Black Magic Woman/Watch Out/ String A Long/Station Man/Did You Ever Love Me/Sentimental Lady/Come A Little Bit Closer/Heroes Are Hard To Find/Trinity/Why

SELECTIONS FROM 25 YEARS – THE CHAIN

Warner Brothers 9362-45188-2
1992
Paper Doll/Love Shines/Love In Store/ Goodbye Angel/Heart Of Stone/Silver Springs/Oh Diane/Big Love/Rhiannon/The Chain/Over My Head/Dreams/Go Your Own Way/Sara/Hold Me/Gypsy/Make Me A Mask/ Don't Stop/Everywhere/Tusk/Not That Funny/Beautiful Child/Teen Beat/Need Your Love So Bad/Did You Ever Love Me/Oh Well (part 1)/I Believe My Time Ain't Long/ Bermuda Triangle/Why/Station Man/ Albatross/Black Magic Woman/Stop Messin' Around/Trinity/Heroes Are Hard To Find/ Green Manalishi

LIVE AT THE BBC

Castle Communications EDF CD 297
1995
Rattlesnake Shake/Sandy Mary/I Believe My Time Ain't Long/Although The Sun Is Shining/Only You/You Never Know What You're Missing/Oh Well/Can't Believe You

Wanna Leave/Jenny Lee/Heavenly/When Will I Be Loved/When I See My Baby/ Buddy's Song/Honey Hush/Preachin'/ Jumping At Shadows/Preachin' Blues/Long Grey Mare/Sweet Home Chicago/Baby Please Set A Date/Blues With A Feeling/Stop Messing Around/Tallahassee Lassie/Hang Onto A Dream/Linda/Mean Mistreating Mama/World Keeps Turning/I Can't Hold Out/Early Morning Come/Albatross/Looking For Somebody/A Fool No More/Got To Move/ Like Crying Like Dying/Man Of The World

TIME

Warner Brothers 9362 45920-2/4
October 1995
Talkin' To My Heart/Hollywood (Some Other Kind Of Town)/Blow By Blow/Winds Of Change/I Do/Nothing Without You/ Dreamin' The Dream/Sooner Or Later/ I Wonder Why/Nights In Estoril/I Got It In For You/All Over Again/These Strange Times

THE DANCE

WEA/Warner Brothers 7599 46702 2
August 1997
The Chain/Dreams/Everywhere/ Rhiannon/I'm So Afraid/Temporary One/ Bleed To Love Her/Big Love/Landslide/Say You Love Me/My Little Demon/Silver Springs/You Make Loving Fun/Sweet Girl/ Go Your Own Way/Tusk/Don't Stop

THE BLUE HORIZON STORY 1965-1970 VOL. 1

Columbia 488992-2
November 1997
This release, compiled by Blue Horizon founder Mike Vernon, is a 3 CD set featuring 70 tracks by 49 artists and is included in the discography as it features the following Fleetwood Mac tracks:
I Believe My Time Ain't Long/Black Magic Woman (different mix)/Need Your Love So Bad/ Albatross
and also includes material by Chicken Shack, Christine Perfect, Eddie Boyd and Otis Spann.

SELECTED BOOTLEGS

MERELY A PORTMANTEAU

1970
Rattlesnake Shake/Underway/Tiger/Green Manalishi/Station Man/Tell Me All The Things You Do

CERULEAN

1985
Madison Blues/Sandy Mary/Stranger Blues/ Great Balls Of Fire/Jenny Jenny/Got To Move/Oh Baby/Teenage Darling/Loving Kind/Tutti Frutti/Rattlesnake Shake/Keep A Knocking/Red Hot Mama/Green Manalishi

LIVE IN LONDON 1968

1989
I Can't Hold Out/Sweet Little Angel/Why Did You Go Away/The World Keeps On Turning/Don't Be Cruel/Oh Well/I Need Your Love/Mean Mistreating Mama/Whole Lotta Love/Talk With You/Bo Diddley/Come Back Baby/Hang Onto A Dream/Sweet Home Chicago/I Got A Mind Of My Own/Mean Old World/Shady Little Baby

LIVE AT THE MARQUEE

1967
Talk To Me Baby/I Held My Baby Last Night/ My Baby's Sweet/Looking For Somebody/Evil Woman Blues/Got To Move/No Place To Go/ Watch Out/Mighty Long Time/Dust My Blues/I Need You, Come On Home/Shake Your Moneymaker

BERMUDA TRIANGLE

1989
Green Manalishi/Angel/Spare Me A Little Of Your Love/Sentimental Lady/Future Games/ Why/Bermuda Triangle/Hypnotized

LIVE IN PASSAIC

1990
Station Man/Spare Me A Little Of Your Love/Rhiannon/Landslide/I'm So Afraid/ World Turning/Don't You Let Me Down Again/Hypnotized

NEXT STOP: MAIN ROAD

1990
The Chain/Dreams/Isn't It Midnight/Oh Well/ Rhiannon/Stop Messin' Round/Save Me/Gold Dust Woman/I Loved Another Woman/ Landslide/World Turning/Everywhere/Stand On The Rock/Little Lies/Stand Back/You Make Loving Fun/Go Your Own Way/Tear It Up/Don't Stop/Gold Dust Woman

WILL THE REAL FLEETWOOD MAC PLEASE STAND UP

Coming Your Way/Green Manalishi/Angel/ Spare Me A Little/Sentimental Lady/Future Games/Bermuda Triangle/Believe Me/Black Magic Woman/Oh Well/Cliff David Blooze/ Rattlesnake Shake/Hypnotized

THEN PLAY ON – BBC BROADCAST

1990
Rattlesnake Shake/Underway/Stranger Blues/ World In Harmony/Tiger/Green Manalishi/ Great Balls Of Fire/Twist And Shout/Whole Lot Of Loving

THE BBC SESSIONS

1989
Need Your Love So Bad/Shake Your Moneymaker/Stop Messin' Round/Long Grey Mare/Baby Please Set A Date/Blues With A Feeling/Tallahassie Lassie/Man Of The World/Jumping At Shadows/Linda/Oh Well/ Rattlesnake Shake/Underway

There are numerous cassette tapes circulating with material ranging from BBC sessions, live concerts from the seventies, eighties and nineties and scores of tapes featuring Stevie Nicks' demos, many of which were intended for various Fleetwood Mac projects. To list all these tapes would be way beyond the scope of this book, in fact it would make a book of its own! To this can be added the many varied compilations that feature The Boston Tea Party material.

SOLO ALBUMS

PETER GREEN

The End Of The Game (Reprise RSLP 9006, 1970)
In The Skies (PVK PVLS 101, 1979)
Little Dreamer (PVK PVLS 102, 1980)
Watcha Gonna Do (PVK PET 1, 1981)
Blue Guitar (Creole CRX 5, 1981)
White Sky (Headline HED 1, 1982)
Kolors (Headline HED 2, 1983)
Come On Down (Homestead HMS 031, 1986)

MICK FLEETWOOD

The Visitor (RCA RCALP 5044, 1981)
I'm Not Me (RCA PL 84652, 1983)
Shakin' The Cage (Capricorn 9362-42004-2, 1992)

JOHN McVIE

John McVie's "Gotta Band" With Lola Thomas (Warners 7599-26909-1/2, 1992)

BOB BRUNNING

Bullen Street Blues (Saga FID 2118, 1969)
Trackside Blues (Saga EROS 8132, 1969)
I Wish You Would (Saga 8150, 1970)
Brunning Hall Sunflower Blues Band (Gemini 2010, 1971)
Live At The Half Moon Putney (Virgin HOT 1, 1981)
A Street Car Named De-Luxe (Appaloosa AP 020, 1981)
Urban De Luxe (Appaloosa AP 040, 1983)
De Luxe Blues Band (Blue Horizon/ACE BLUH 004, 1988)
Motorvating (Appaloosa 1220601, 1988)

CHRISTINE PERFECT (McVIE)

Christine Perfect (Blue Horizon 7-63860, 1970)
Christine McVie (Warners 925 059-1, 1984)

JEREMY SPENCER

Jeremy Spencer (Reprise RSLP 9002, 1970)
Jeremy Spencer And The Children Of God (CBS 65387, 1973)
Flee (Atlantic K 50624, 1979)

DANNY KIRWAN

Second Chapter (DJM DJLPS 454, 1975)
Midnight In San Juan (DJM DJF 20481, 1976)
Hello There Big Boy (DJM DJF 20555, 1979)

BOB WELCH

Paris (Capitol EST 11464, 1976)
Big Town 2061 (Capitol EST 11560, 1976)
French Kiss (Capitol EST 11663, 1977)
Three Hearts (Capitol EST 11907, 1979)
The Other One (Capitol EST 12017, 1980)
Bob Welch (RCA RCALP 6019, 1982)

BUCKINGHAM/NICKS

Buckingham Nicks (Polydor 2391 093, 1977)

LINDSEY BUCKINGHAM

Law And Order (Mercury 6302 167, 1981)
Go Insane (Mercury MERL 46, 1984)
Out Of The Cradle (Mercury 512658, 1992)

STEVIE NICKS

Bella Donna (WEA K 99169, 1981)
The Wild Heart (WEA 2500711, 1983)
Rock A Little (Parlophone PCS 7300, 1985)
The Other Side Of The Mirror (EMIEMD 1008, 1989)
Time Space: The Best Of Stevie Nicks (EMIEMD 1024, 1991)
Street Angel (92246-2)

RICK VITO

King Of Hearts (Modern Records 7-91789, 1992)

BILLY BURNETTE

Billy Burnette (Entrance Z 31228, 1972)
Between Friends (Polydor 2391436, 1979)
Billy Burnette (Columbia JC 36792, 1980)
Gimme You (CBS 87460, 1981)
Try Me (MCA/CURB MCA5604, 1985)
Soldier Of Love (MCA 5768, 1986)

VIDEOS

FLEETWOOD MAC DOCUMENTARY

Warner Home Video PEV 4022
1981
Sisters Of The Moon/Walk A Thin Line/
Angel/Save Me A Place/Tusk/Songbird/The
Chain/Go Your Own Way/Never Make Me
Cry/Sara/Think About Me/Not That Funny

IN CONCERT – MIRAGE TOUR 1982

RCA RVT 10134
1984
The Chain/Gypsy/Love In Store/Not That
Funny/You Make Loving Fun/I'm So Afraid/
Blue Letter/Rhiannon/Tusk/Eyes Of The
World/Go Your Own Way/Sisters Of The
Moon/Songbird

TANGO IN THE NIGHT

Warners Home Video 9381493
1988
The Chain/Everywhere/Dreams/Seven
Wonders/Isn't It Midnight/World Turning/
Little Lies/Oh Well/Gold Dust Woman/
Another Woman/Stand Back/Songbird/
Don't Stop

THE EARLY YEARS 1967–1970

PNEVideo 1008
1995
Black Magic Woman/Heart Beat Like A
Hammer/Shake Your Moneymaker/I'm
Worried/Like It This Way/World Keep On
Turning/Stop Messin' Round/Albatross/Need
Your Love So Bad/Man Of The World/Like
Crying/Linda/Oh Well/Rattlesnake Shake/
Green Manalishi

THE DANCE

Warners Home Video 7599 38486-3
1997
The Chain/Dreams/Everywhere/Rhiannon/
I'm So Afraid/Temporary One/Bleed To Love
Her/Big Love/Landslide/Say You Love Me/My
Little Demon/Silver Springs/You Make
Loving Fun/Sweet Girl/Go Your Own Way/
Tusk/Don't Stop/Songbird

CLASSIC ALBUMS - FLEETWOOD MAC RUMOURS

Eagle Rock Entertainment CLASS 102
September 1997
The definitive story of the making of
Fleetwood Mac's RUMOURS with contributions
from Lindsey Buckingham, Mick Fleetwood,
Christine McVie, John McVie, Stevie Nicks,
Ken Caillat and Richard Dashut. Includes a
specially recorded version of Christine
McVie's 'Songbird' and an acoustic version of
'Never Going Back Again' by Lindsey
Buckingham.

Chart Statistics

UK CHART STATISTICS

SINGLES

I Believe My Time Ain't Long	—
Black Magic Woman	37
Need Your Love So Bad	31
Albatross	1
Man Of The World	2
Need Your Love So Bad (Re-issue)	32
Oh Well	2
The Green Manalishi	10
Albatross (Re-issue)	2
Spare Me A Little	—
Did You Ever Love Me	—
For Your Love	—
Heroes Are Hard To Find	—
Warm Ways	—
Over My Head	—
Rhiannon	—
Say You Love Me	40
Go Your Own Way	38
Don't Stop	32
Dreams	24
You Make Loving Fun	45
Rhiannon	46
Tusk	6
Sara	37
Not That Funny	—
Think About Me	—
The Farmer's Daughter	—
Hold Me	—
Gypsy	46
Oh Diane	9
Can't Go Back	—
Big Love	9
Seven Wonders	56
Little Lies	5
Family Man	54
Everywhere	4
Isn't It Midnight	60
As Long As You Follow	66
Hold Me	—
Save Me	53
Skies The Limit	—
In The Back Of My Mind	58
Love Shines	—

ALBUMS

Peter Green's Fleetwood Mac	4
Mr Wonderful	10
Pious Bird Of Good Omen	18
Then Play On	6
Blues Jam At Chess	—
Kiln House	39
The Original Fleetwood Mac	—
Future Games	—
Bare Trees	—
Penguin	—
Mystery To Me	—
Heroes Are Hard To Find	—
Greatest Hits	36
Fleetwood Mac	23
Rumours	1
Tusk	1
Fleetwood Mac Live	31
Mirage	5
Tango In The Night	1

Greatest Hits	3
Behind The Mask	1
Live At The BBC	48
Time	47
The Dance	14

US CHART STATISTICS

SINGLES

I Believe My Time Ain't Long	—
Black Magic Woman	—
Need Your Love So Bad	—
Albatross	—
Man Of The World	—
Oh Well	55
The Green Manalishi	—
Jewel Eyed Judy	—
Dragonfly	—
Sands Of Time	—
Spare Me A Little	—
Did You Ever Love Me	—
For Your Love	—
Heroes Are Hard To Find	—
Over My Head	20
Rhiannon	11
Say You Love Me	11
Go Your Own Way	10
Dreams	1
Don't Stop	3
You Make Loving Fun	9
Tusk	8
Sara	7
Think About Me	20
Sisters Of The Moon	86
Fireflies	60
Hold Me	4
Gypsy	12
Love In Store	22
Big Love	5
Seven Wonders	19
Little Lies	4
Everywhere	14
Family Man	90
As Long As You Follow	43
Save Me	33
Silver Springs	—

ALBUMS

Peter Green's Fleetwood Mac	198
Mr Wonderful	—
English Rose	184
Then Play On	109
Kiln House	69
Fleetwood Mac In Chicago	190
Black Magic Woman	143
Future Games	91
Bare Trees	70
Penguin	49
Mystery To Me	67
Heroes Are Hard To Find	34
Vintage Years	138
Fleetwood Mac	1
Fleetwood Mac In Chicago (re-issue)	118
Rumours	1
Tusk	4
Fleetwood Mac Live	14
Mirage	1
Tango In The Night	7
Greatest Hits	14
Behind The Mask	18
Live At The BBC	—
Time	—
The Dance	1

Awards

GRAMMY NOMINATIONS AND AWARDS

1977   Nominated for Album of the Year
RUMOURS – **Winner**

Nominated for Best Pop
Performance By A Duo, Group
or Chorus with Vocal
RUMOURS

Nominated for Best Arrangement
for Voices
'Go Your Own Way'

ROLLING STONE AWARDS

1977   Artists Of The Year
Fleetwood Mac

Band Of The Year
Fleetwood Mac

Best Album
RUMOURS

Best Single
'Dreams'

AMERICAN MUSIC AWARDS

1978   Favourite Band
Fleetwood Mac – **Winner**

Favourite Album
RUMOURS – **Winner**

SILVER, GOLD AND PLATINUM AWARDS FROM THE BRITISH PHONOGRAPHIC INSTITUTE

Albums	RUMOURS	Platinum x 7
	TANGO IN THE NIGHT	Platinum x 7
	GREATEST HITS	Platinum x 3
	BEHIND THE MASK	Platinum
	TUSK	Platinum
	THE COLLECTION	Gold
	FLEETWOOD MAC	Gold
	FLEETWOOD MAC LIVE	Gold
	MIRAGE	Gold
Singles	'Tusk'	Silver
	'Albatross'	Silver

GOLD AND PLATINUM AWARDS FROM THE RECORD INDUSTRY ASSOCIATION OF AMERICA

Album	RUMOURS	Platinum x 17
	FLEETWOOD MAC	Platinum x 5
	GREATEST HITS	Platinum x 4
	TANGO IN THE NIGHT	Platinum x 2
	TUSK	Platinum x 2
	MIRAGE	Platinum x 2
	THE DANCE	Platinum x42
	BARE TREES	Platinum
	MYSTERY TO ME	Gold
	BEHIND THE MASK	Gold
	FLEETWOOD MAC LIVE	Gold
Singles	'Dreams'	Gold
Video	*Tango In The Night*	Gold
	The Dance	Gold

Song Title Index

24 Karat (Nicks) 67

(I'm) A Road Runner (Holland/Dozier/
 Holland) 54
A Fool No More (Green) 20, 22
A Mind Of My Own (Unknown) 32
A Talk With You (Unknown) 32
Affairs Of The Heart (Nicks) 84
Ain't Nobody's Business (Grainger/Williams/
 Prince) 38, 42
Albatross (Green) 32, 35, 43, 44
All Over Again (McVie/Quintela) 44, 91
Allow Me One More Show (Spencer) 22
Although The Sun Is Shining (Kirwan) 44, 45
Angel (Welch) 57
Angel (Nicks) 67, 70
As Long As You Follow (Unknown) 82

Baby Don't You Want To Go (Unknown) 35
Baby Please Set A Date (McCoy) 20, 35
Bad Loser (McVie) 57
Bare Trees (Kirwan) 52
Be Careful (Unknown) 26
Beautiful Child (Nicks) 67
Bee-I-Bicky-Bop-Blue-Jean-Honey-Babe-Meets-
 High-School-Hound-Dog-Hot-Rod-Man
 (Unknown) 25
Before The Beginning (Green) 44
Behind The Mask (McVie) 85
Believe Me (McVie) 54
Bermuda Triangle (Welch) 57, 58
Big Love (Buckingham) 78, 80, 93
Black Jack Blues (Brown) 38
Black Magic Woman (Green) 26, 27, 45

Black Slack (Unknown) 26
Bleed To Love Her (Buckingham) 93
Bleeding Heart (Unknown) 27
Blood On The Floor (Spencer) 48
Blow By Blow (Mason/Cesario/Holden) 91
Blue Coat Man (Unknown) 25
Blue Letter (Curtis) 59, 76
Blue Suede Shoes (Perkins) 44
Blues For Hippies (Unknown) 42
Blues With A Feeling (Jacobs) 43
Bobby's Blues (Unknown) 37
Bo Diddley (Unknown) 32
Book Of Love (Buckingham/Dashut) 75, 76
Book Of Miracles (Unknown) 80, 81
Born Enchanter (Welch) 57
Bright Fire (Welch) 54
Brown Eyes (McVie) 66, 93
Buddy's Song (Holly) 48
Buzz Me (Unknown) 27, 28

Can't Afford To Do It (Williamson) 22
Can't Go Back (Buckingham) 75, 76
Can't Help Falling In Love (Peretti, Creatore,
 Weiss) 78
Caroline (Buckingham) 78, 80
Caught In The Rain (Weston) 54
Cecilia (Unknown) 67
Child Of Mine (Kirwan) 52
Close My Eyes (Green) 44
Cold Black Night (Spencer) 22
Come A Little Bit Closer (McVie) 57
Coming Home (James) 28
Coming Home (Welch) 57
Coming Your Way (Kirwan) 44, 45

Cool Clear Water (Nolan) 75, 76
Crazy About You Baby (Unknown) 35, 49
Crazy For My Baby (Unknown) 32
Crutch And Cane (Unknown) 32
Crystal (Nicks) 59

Danny's Chant (Kirwan) 52
Dead Shrimp Blues (Unknown) 32
Did You Ever Love Me (McVie/Welch) 54
Dig You (Spann) 42
Dissatisfied (McVie) 54
Do You Know (Burnette/McVie) 84
Doctor Brown (Brown) 28
Don't Be Cruel (Blackwell/Presley) 25
Don't Dog Me (Unknown) 23
Don't Know Which Way To Go (Unknown) 27
Don't Let Me Down Again (Buckingham) 61,
    66, 70
Don't Stop (McVie) 63, 65, 70, 84, 87, 90, 93
Double Trouble (Unknown) 15
Down At The Crown For Now (Unknown)
    49, 50
Down Endless Street (Unknown) 80, 81
Dragonfly (Kirwan/Davies) 49, 50
Dreamin' The Dream (Bramlett/Burnette) 91
Dreams (Nicks) 63, 65, 69, 70, 82, 87, 93
Drifting (Green) 27
Dust (Kirwan) 52
Dust My Blues (Johnson) 19
Dust My Broom (Johnson) 28, 44

Earl Gray (Kirwan) 48
Early Morning Come (Kirwan) 43
Emerald Eyes (Welch) 54
Empire State (Buckingham/Dashut) 75, 76
Evenin' Boogie (Spencer) 29
Everyday I Have The Blues (Chatman) 38
Everywhere (McVie) 78, 80, 82, 84, 87, 93
Evil Woman Blues (Green) 19
Eyes Of The World (Buckingham) 75, 76, 78

Family Man (Buckingham/Dashut) 78, 80
Family Party (Bonus Beats) 80, 81
Farmer's Daughter (Wilson/Love) 71
Fighting For Madge (Fleetwood) 44
Fireflies (Nicks) 71
First Train Home (Green) 15
Fleetwood Mac (Green) 15
For Your Love (Gouldman) 55
Forbidden (Unknown) 93

Forever (Weston/McVie/Welch) 54
Freedom (Nicks/Campbell) 85
Future Games (Welch) 52, 58

Get Like You Used To Be (Unknown) 50
Go Insane (Buckingham) 93
Go Your Own Way (Buckingham) 63, 65, 70,
    73, 78, 87, 93
Gold Dust Woman (Nicks) 63, 84, 87, 93
Good Things (Unknown) 55
Goodbye Angel (Buckingham) 75, 76
Got To Move (Williamson) 19, 20, 22, 27,
    44, 46
Great Balls Of Fire (Blackwell/Hammer) 46, 47
Gypsy (Nicks) 75, 76, 93

Hang Onto A Dream (Hardin) 35
Hard Feelings (Burnette/Silbar) 85
Hard To Resist (Unknown) 30
Hard-Headed Woman (DeMetrius) 35
Have A Good Time (Unknown) 37, 38
Heart Of Stone (McVie/Quintela) 89
Heavenly (Unknown) 43
Hellhound On My Trail (Trad. Arr. Green) 22
Heroes Are Hard To Find (McVie) 57
Hi Ho Silver (Waller/Kirkeby) 48
Hold Me (McVie/Patton) 75, 76
Hollywood (Some Other Kind Of Town)
    (McVie/Quintela) 91
Homeward Bound (McVie) 52
Homework (Perkins/Clark) 38
Honey Hi (McVie) 67
Honey Hush (Turner) 48
Horton's Boogie Woogie (Unknown) 37
Hot Rodding (Unknown) 43
How Blue Can You Get (Unknown) 27, 28
Hungry Country Girl (Spann) 38
Hypnotized (Welch) 54, 58, 61

I Believe My Time Ain't Long (James) 18, 20
I Can't Believe You Want To Leave (Price) 43
I Can't Hold On (James) 25, 43
I Can't Hold Out (James) 37, 44
(I Can't Stop) Loving You (Unknown) 26
I Do (McVie/Quintela) 91
I Don't Want To Know (Nicks) 63
I Got It In For You (Burnette/Allen) 91
I Got The Blues (Horton) 38
I Have To Laugh (Unknown) 32
I Held My Baby Last Night (James) 19, 27, 37

I Know I'm Not Wrong (Buckingham) 67, 70
I Loved Another Woman (Green) 22, 84, 87
I Need Some Air (Spann) 42
I Need You, Come On Home (Spencer) 19
I Need Your Love (Horton) 37
I Wonder Why (Mason/Previte/Fuller) 91
I'm So Afraid (Buckingham) 59, 60, 70, 73,
    76, 93
I'm So Lonesome And Blue (Unknown) 28
I'm Worried (James) 37
I've Lost My Baby (Spencer) 29
If You Be My Baby (Green/Adams) 28, 32
If You Ever Did Believe (Unknown) 63
If You Were My Love (Unknown) 75
In The Back Of My Mind (Burnette/Malloy)
    84, 85
In The City (Welch) 55
Instrumental (Unknown) 37, 38
Instrumental (Uptempo) (Unknown) 37
Intergalactic Musicians Walking On Velvet
    (Unknown) 32
Isn't It Midnight (McVie/Quintela/Buckingham)
    78, 81, 82, 87
It Hurts Me Too (Unknown) 15
It Was A Big Thing (Spann) 42

Jenny Lee (Spencer) 48
Jenny, Jenny (Unknown) 46
Jewel Eyed Judy (Kirwan/Fleetwood/McVie)
    48
Jigsaw Puzzle Blues (Kirwan) 32
Juliet (Nicks) 80, 81
Jumping At Shadows (Bennett) 45
Just Crazy Love (McVie) 54
Just The Blues (Boyd) 26
Just Want To Tell You (Unknown) 44

Keep On Going (Welch) 54
Keep-A-Knocking (Unknown) 46

Lady From The Mountain (Unknown) 67
Landslide (Nicks) 59, 60, 70, 87, 93
Last Night (Jacobs) 37
Lay It All Down (Welch) 52
Lazy Poker Blues (Green/Adams) 29
Leaving Town Blues (Green) 23, 47
Like Crying Like Dying (Kirwan) 35, 44
Like It This Way (Kirwan) 38, 45
Linda (Spencer) 45
Little Lies (McVie/Quintela) 78, 80, 84, 87, 93

Lizard People (Unknown) 85
Long Grey Mare (Green) 18, 20, 28
Looking For Somebody (Green) 19, 20, 22
Love In Store (McVie/Recor) 75, 76
Love Is Dangerous (Vito/Nicks) 84
Love Shines (McVie/Quintela) 89
Love That Burns (Green/Adams) 28
Love That Woman (Leake) 27
Loving Kind (Unknown) 46

Madison Blues (James) 37, 46
Make Me A Mask (Buckingham) 75, 76
Man Of The World (Green) 43, 45
Mean Mistreatin' Mama (Carr) 32
Mean Old Fireman (Trad. Arr. Spencer) 22
Merry Go Round (Green) 22, 44
Mighty Long Time (Williamson) 19
Miles Away (Welch) 55
Mission Bell (Michael/Hodges) 48
Monday Morning (Buckingham) 59, 65, 70
Morning Rain (McVie) 52
My Baby Is Sweet (Williamson) 19, 27, 28
My Baby's A Good Un (Unknown) 27
My Baby's Gone (Unknown) 38
My Baby's Good To Me (Spencer) 22
My Dream (Kirwan) 44
My Heart Beat Like A Hammer (Spencer) 22
My Little Demon (Buckingham) 93
My Love Depends On You (Spann) 42
Mystified (Buckingham/McVie) 78, 80

Need Your Love So Bad (John) 27, 29, 30, 32,
    35
Need Your Love Tonight (Spencer) 28
Never Forget (McVie) 67
Never Going Back Again (Buckingham) 63, 73,
    93
Never Make Me Cry (McVie) 67
New Worried Blues (Unknown) 43
Nights In Estoril (McVie/Quintela) 91
Nightwatch (Welch) 54
No More Doggin' (Gordon/Taub) 42
No Place To Go (Burnett) 19, 22
No Questions Asked (Unknown) 82
Not That Funny (Buckingham) 67, 69, 73, 76
Nothing Without You (Bramlett/Gillmore/
    Bramlett) 91

Oh Daddy (McVie) 63, 70
Oh Diane (Buckingham/Dashut) 75, 76

Oh Well (Part 1) (Green) 44, 45, 65, 69, 70, 84, 87
Oh Well (Part 2) (Green) 44
One More Night (McVie) 71
One Sided Love (Unknown) 44
One Sunny Day (Kirwan) 35
One Together (Spencer) 48
Only Over You (McVie) 75, 76
Only You (McVie) 45, 47
Ooh Baby (Burnett) 37, 46
Out On The Road (Unknown) 67
Over And Over (McVie) 66, 69, 72
Over My Head (McVie) 59, 65, 73, 93

Paper Doll (Nicks/Vito/Herron) 89
Peggy Sue Got Married (Holly) 27, 43
Please Find My Baby (Unknown) 27
Preachin' (Turner) 50
Preachin' Blues (Unknown) 32
Prove Your Love (McVie) 57
Purple Dancer (Fleetwood/McVie/Kirwan) 49, 50

Rambling Pony (Green) 18
Rambling Pony #2 (Green) 18
Rattlesnake Shake (Green) 44, 46
Red Hot Jam (Green) 37
Red Hot Mama (James) 46
Remember Me (McVie) 54
Revelation (Welch) 54
Rhiannon (Nicks) 59, 60, 65, 69, 70, 76, 87, 93
Ricky (Unknown) 80, 81
Rock Me Baby (Unknown) 38
Rockin' Boogie (Spencer) 38
Roll Along Blues (Unknown) 43
Rollin' Man (Green/Adams) 28

Safe Harbour (Welch) 57
San Ho Zay (Unknown) 44
Sands Of Time (Kirwan) 52
Sandy Mary (Green) 46, 47, 49
Sara (Nicks) 66, 69, 70
Save Me (McVie/Quintela) 84, 87
Save Me A Place (Buckingham) 66, 70
Say You Love Me (McVie) 59, 70, 72, 93
Searching For Madge (McVie) 44
Second Hand News (Buckingham) 63, 93
Sent For You Yesterday And Here You Come Today (Basie/Durham/Rushing) 26
Sentimental Lady (Welch) 52, 58

Seven Wonders (Stewart/Nicks) 78, 80, 82
Shadows Of Love (Nicks) 93
Shady Little Baby (Unknown) 43
Shake Your Moneymaker (James) 19, 23
She's Changing Me (Welch) 57
She's Gone (Unknown) 26
She's Real (Unknown) 26
She Needs Some Loving (Spann) 42
Sheila (Unknown) 32
Show Me A Smile (McVie) 52
Show-Biz Blues (Green) 44
Silver Heels (Welch) 57
Silver Springs (Nicks) 63, 93
Sisters Of The Moon (Nicks) 67, 70, 78
Skies The Limit (McVie/Quintela) 84
Smile At You #1 (Nicks) 75
Smile At You #2 (Nicks) 75
Somebody (Welch) 55
Somebody's Gonna Get Their Head Kicked In Tonight (Spencer) 43
Someday Baby (Estes/Nixon) 42
Someday Soon Baby (Unknown) 38
Something Inside Of Me (Kirwan) 35
Sometimes (Kirwan) 52
Songbird (McVie) 65, 70, 78, 84, 93
Sooner Or Later (McVie/Quintela) 91
South Indiana-1 (Horton) 37
South Indiana-2 (Horton) 37
Spare Me A Little Of Your Love (McVie) 52, 58, 60
Stand On The Rock (Vito) 85, 87
Standback (Nicks) 84, 87
Start Again (Unknown) 50
Station Man (Kirwan/Spencer/McVie) 48, 50, 60
Stop Messin' Round (Green/Adams) 29, 44, 87
Storms (Nicks) 67
Straight Back (Nicks) 75, 76
Stranger Blues (Unknown) 46, 47
Sugar Daddy (McVie) 59
Sugar Mama (Burnett) 38, 44
Sunny Side Of Heaven (Kirwan) 52
Sweet Girl (Nicks) 93
Sweet Home Chicago (Johnson) 35
Sweet Little Angel (Unknown) 25

Talk To Me Baby (James) 19
Talk With You (Kirwan) 38, 44
Talkin' To My Heart (Burnette/Allen/VanHoy) 91
Tallahassie Lassie (Slay/Picariello/Crewe) 43

Tango In The Night (Buckingham) 78, 80
Teen Beat (Buckingham/Dashut) 75, 76
Teenage Darling (Spencer) 46, 50
Tear It Up (Unknown) 87
Tell Me All The Things You Do (Kirwan) 48, 49
Temperature Is Rising (98.8°F) (Spann) 42
Temperature Is Rising (100.2°F) (Spann) 42
Temporary One (McVie/Quintela) 93
Ten To One (Unknown) 26
Thank You Baby (Unknown) 26
That Ain't It (Unknown) 32
That's All For Everyone (Buckingham) 67
That's Alright (Nicks) 75, 76
That's Enough For Me (Buckingham) 67
The Big Boat (Boyd) 26
The Blues Is Here To Stay (Unknown) 26
The Chain (Buckingham/Nicks/McVie/
    Fleetwood/McVie) 63, 65, 69, 76, 82, 84,
    85, 93
The Dealer (Nicks) 67
The Derelict (Walker) 54
The Dream (Unknown) 27
The Ghost (Welch) 52
The Green Manalishi (Green) 46, 47, 57
The Ledge (Buckingham) 66, 69
The Second Time (Nicks/Vito) 85
The Stroller (Unknown) 25
The Sun Is Shining (James) 25, 27
The Way I Feel (McVie) 55
The World Keep On Turning (Green) 22, 27
These Strange Times (Fleetwood/Kennedy) 91
Think About It (Nicks) 63
Think About Me (McVie) 66
Third Degree (Unknown) 26
This Is The Rock (Spencer) 48
Thoughts On A Grey Day (Mrs Scarrot) 52
Tiger (Unknown) 47
Trinity (Kirwan) 52
Trying So Hard To Forget (Green/Adams) 29
Turn Me Loose (Pomus/Shuman) 49
Tusk (Buckingham) 67, 68, 70, 76, 93
Tutti Frutti (LaBostrie/Penniman) 46
Twist And Shout (Russel/Medley) 47
Twisted (Unknown) 93

Under Way (Green) 44, 47

Walk A Thin Line (Buckingham) 67
Walkin' (Spann) 42
Warm Ways (McVie) 59
Watch Out (Green) 19, 22, 37
Watchdevil (Nicks) 67
Welcome To The Room . . . Sara (Nicks) 78, 80
What A Shame (Welch/Fleetwood/Kirwan/
    McVie/McVie) 52
What Has Rock And Roll Ever Done For You
    (Nicks) 81
What Makes You Think You're The One
    (Buckingham) 67, 69
When I See My Baby (Kirwan) 48
When I See You Again (Nicks) 78, 81
When It Comes To Love (Burnette/Morgan/
    Climie) 85
When The Sun Goes Down (Vito/Burnette)
    85
When Will I Be Loved (Everly) 48
When You Say (Kirwan) 44
Where Were You (Unknown) 93
Where You Belong (Unknown) 25, 27
Why (McVie) 55, 58
Winds Of Change (Hain) 91
Wine, Whiskey, Women (Unknown) 32
Wish You Were Here (McVie/Allen) 75, 76
Without You (Kirwan) 35
Woman Of A Thousand Years (Kirwan) 52
World In Harmony (Kirwan/Green) 45, 47
World Keeps Turning (Green) 25, 27
World Turning (McVie/Buckingham) 59, 60, 65,
    70, 84, 87
World's In A Tangle (Lane) 38
Worried Dream (King) 27

You And I, Part I (Buckingham/McVie) 78, 81
You And I, Part II (Buckingham/McVie) 78, 81
You Are My Love (Unknown) 26
You Make Loving Fun (McVie) 63, 70, 76, 87,
    93
You Got To Reap (Unknown) 26
You Need Love (Unknown) 32
You'll Be Mine (Unknown) 43
You'll Never Know What You're Missing Till
    You Try (Spencer) 43
You're The One (Unknown) 32

PICTURE CREDITS

The author and publisher would like to thank the following for supplying illustrations and acknowledge the relevant record companies for the reproduction of album covers, etc.:

All Action 13 (Dave Hogan), 80–1 and 84 (Justin Thomas), 85 (Laurence Estrew), 88 (Steve Douglas), 89 (Justin Thomas), 90 (left), 90 (right) (Duncan Raban), 92 (bottom) (Justin Thomas); **Baktabak Collectors Editions** 69; **Nancy Barr-Brandon** 66, 68, 82, 91 (right); **Max Browne/Dave Peabody** 14; **Bob Brunning** 6, 17 (bottom); **Castle Communications** 34 (bottom) (Chris Walker/Ross Halfin), 36 (Chris Walker/Ross Halfin), 46, 92 (top) (Chris Walker/Ross Halfin); **Channel 5 Video** 77; **Fleetwood Tours** 83; **Record Plant** 97; **Mike Ross-Trevor** 96, 98; **SGRS Records** 61; **Sony Music** 18–31, 33, 34 (top), 39–40, 41 (right) (Terence Ibbott), 41 (left) (Jeff Lowenthal), 42 (Terence Ibbott), 51; **Sound City Studios** 59; **Sunset Sound** 91 (left); **Warner Brothers** 1, 8, 53–4, 55 (Clive Arrowsmith), 56 (Herbert Worthington), 62, 64, 67, 72; **Warner Brothers/IMP** 74; **Warner/Reprise** 86, 94, 95 (David LaChapelle).

Every effort has been made to acknowledge correctly and contact the source and/or copyright holder of each illustration, and we apologize for any unintentional errors or omissions, which will be rectified in any future editions of the book.

AUTHOR'S NOTE

At the time of going to press, this new compilation has been released, which features 31 previously unreleased studio jams and alternate versions of tracks recorded between 1968 and 1970. Fifteen have never been issued in any form while the remaining tracks are alternate versions. While it was too late to add the relevant details to the main part of this book, the details have been included here to ensure the accuracy of the book.

THE VAUDEVILLE YEARS OF FLEETWOOD MAC 1968–1970

Receiver Records RDPCD014
September 1998
Intro-Lazy Poker Blues (unissued version)/My Baby's Sweeter (unissued version)/Love That Burns (unissued version)/Talk To Me Baby (unissued version)/Everyday I Have The Blues (unissued version)/Jeremy's Contribution To Doo Wop (previously unissued)/Everyday I Have The Blues (unissued version)/Death Bells (previously unissued)/(Watch Out For Yourself) Mr Jones (previously unissued)/Man Of Action (previously unissued)/Do You Give A Damn For Me (unissued version)/Man Of The World (unissued version)/Like It This Way (unissued version)/Blues In B Flat Minor (unissued instrumental)/Someone's Gonna Get Their Head Kicked In Tonight (full length version)/Although The Sun Is Shining (unissued version) Showbiz Blues (unissued version)/Underway (full length version)/The Madge Session Part 1 (unissued instrumental) The Madge Session Part 2 (unissued instrumental)/(That's What) I Want You To Know (previously unissued)/Oh Well (alternate version)/Love It Seems (previously unissued)/Mighty Cold (previously unissued)/Fast Talking Woman Blues (unissued instrumental)/Tell Me From The Start (previously unissued)/October Jam Part 1 (unissued instrumental)/October Jam Part 2 (unissued instrumental)/Green Manalishi (unissued version)/World In Harmony (unissued version)/Farewell (unissued demo).